Editor
Lorin Klistoff, M.A.

Editor in Chief
Karen J. Goldfluss, M.S. Ed.

Illustrator
Teacher Created Resources

Cover Artist
Marilyn Goldberg

Art Coordinator
Renée Christine Yates

Art Manager
Kevin Barnes

Imaging
Craig Gunnell

Publisher
Mary D. Smith, M.S. Ed.

Joni Taylor

Author

Robert W. Smith

Teacher Created Resources, Inc.
12621 Western Avenue
Garden Grove, CA 92841
www.teachercreated.com

ISBN: 978-1-4206-3999-5

Reprinted, 2019

Made in U.S.A.

TABLE OF CONTENTS

TABLE OF CONTENTS

What is Readers' Theater?

Readers' theater is drama without the need for costumes, props, stage, or memorization. It is done in the classroom by groups of students who become the cast of the dramatic reading. The players employ their oral reading skills, creative expression, and dramatic voice to communicate the mood and the meaning of the script. Students should have practiced the script several times over a few days, be well versed in the meaning of the text, and be well practiced in using correct pronunciation, proper voice inflection, appropriate changes in volume, and various nuances of expression to create an effective dramatic reading. They should also understand the historical context of the readings.

Why Use Readers' Theater in Social Studies?

Children need to live history. A steady diet of textbook readings and vague focus questions tends to make history a series of meaningless, disconnected events. The vibrant story of recorded human history becomes dry, tasteless, and boring. Students need to have a sense of involvement with the human dramas that make up the history of men and women down through the ages. Children can relate to the fiery devastation of Pompeii and the terror it created among children their own age. They can imagine the excitement of discovery as Archimedes conceives the displacement of water and Eratosthenes deduces the circumference of Earth. They can get a glimpse of the creativity and imagination of those two scientists and the intellectual acuity of Socrates.

Students will better comprehend the complex motivations and personal struggles of individuals affected by the political and religious conflicts that rocked the eras of Hatshepsut, Hypatia, Alexander, Esther, Qin Shi Huangdi, and Cleopatra. They will be astonished and disturbed by the inequalities and prejudices of the ancient world in all cultures as diverse as the civilizations of China, Greece, Rome, and Babylon.

Students will recognize the seeds of their own American culture in the laws, customs, desires, and ideals of Hammurabi, Socrates, Caesar, Esther, and Hypatia. The birth of science and learning flows from the work of Archimedes and Eratosthenes and their ancient counterparts. Using readers' theater and other dramatic activities is a creative way to grab student imagination and focus it on a period of history.

Literature Connections

The stories that unfold in these readers' theater scripts can be the spark that lights student interest in some of the best children's historical literature and biography. Biographies of Julius Caesar, Cleopatra, Mark Antony, Hatshepsut, and Alexander the Great offer students a guided tour through the civilizations and cultures of ancient times. Readers can discern the ideas and motivations of scientists, generals, kings, and emperors. Other historical texts guide students through the streets of Pompeii, the thought processes of Archimedes and Eratosthenes, Alexander's lust for conquest, Caesar's relentless ambition, and Cleopatra's subtle manipulation of powerful men. Many units in this book highlight effective and engaging works of children's biography and literature to help extend the lesson.

Portraying Dramatic History

Children become more involved in historical events when they immerse themselves in the action. Having children create scripts based on the historical characters they are studying is a good way of motivating students to think about historical events and consider the consequences of individual human actions and cultural interactions. Encourage students to use the dramatic format and the suggestions in each extension activity to create their own readers' theater scripts. The art suggestions in many units help students visualize the personalities of the individuals highlighted in the dramatic texts. The suggestions indicate simple, easily attainable art materials to use in creating maps, portraits, and models. Use the discussion activities on the last page of each unit to help students internalize the motives of the characters in the scripts or to draw closure after the script has been performed.

Targeting the Topics

You will want to use the scripts in this book as you teach individual civilizations in ancient history. There are representative scripts for periods beginning with the Babylonian empire and continuing through Egyptian, Greek, Roman, Chinese, and Hebrew civilizations. The focus of the scripts varies from scientists, mathematicians, and philosophers to kings, queens, and emperors, to warriors and common men and women. In this span of more than 2,200 years from Hammurabi to Hypatia are topics as diverse as the development of written laws, the foundations of scientific inquiry, the growth and decline of great civilizations, the rights of individual citizens, the absolute power of rulers, and the effects of natural disasters on people and cultures.

Working with the Scripts

Each script is designed to illuminate one facet or significant event in the historical sweep of a given era. The background information preceding each script gives a brief historical context to help your students place the event in terms of time and place. Depending upon circumstances, you may want to do several scripts simultaneously with your class as you finish a semester of work, or do the scripts along the way as you finish individual topics in ancient history. Teachers whose time for teaching history in the upper elementary grades is limited may choose to use these scripts and the background information as the primary vehicle for social studies instruction and reinforce these tools with selected textbook readings or high quality historical fiction and children's biography. (**Note to the Teacher:** It is important to review the content of each script prior to classroom study. Choose scripts that are appropriate to your curriculum and are suitable for your students.)

Selecting Teams and Leaders

If all of your class will be doing readers' theater dramatic readings, select good readers and effective leaders for each script. These leaders will often do the narration or provide a strong voice for one of the longer or more important dramatic parts. They should help resolve some questions of pronunciation and the meanings for words that are unfamiliar to some of the students. You will also need to assist teams with these tasks and resolve occasional disputes related to meaning or role selection.

INTRODUCTION *(cont.)*

Selecting Teams and Leaders *(cont.)*

Assign each of the student script leaders a team composed of students with varying reading abilities. You may want shy children, struggling readers, or students just learning English to have more limited roles in their first readers' theater experiences. However, all students should have ample time to practice with their fellow team members so that the performance is effective and interesting to the student audience.

Staging

The classroom is the stage. Place the proper number (four to seven) stools, chairs, or desks to sit on in a semicircle at the front of your class or in a separate staging area. You may use simple costumes, but generally no costume is expected or used in this type of dramatization. If you have plain robes or simple coats of the same color or style so that everyone looks about the same, this can have a nice effect. Students dressed in the same school uniform or colors create an atmosphere of seriousness. Props are not needed, but they may be used for additional effects.

Scripting

Each member of your group should have a clearly marked, useable script, as well as the complete unit with background information, extensions, and discussion questions. Students should be able to personalize the script with notes indicating when they speak, which part or parts they are reading, and mechanical notes about pronunciation of specific words and phrases or sentences they intend to emphasize in some dramatic way.

Performing

Students should enter the classroom quietly and seriously. They should sit silently and unmoving on the stools or chairs. Performers should wait with heads lowered, or they should focus on an object above the audience. When the narrator starts the reading, the actors can then focus on their scripts. The actors should look at whoever is reading, except when they are performing.

Movement, Memorization, and Mime

Experienced readers' theater actors may add gestures or other movements to their lines. Some actors may choose to introduce mime to a performance if it seems to fit. Several actors will learn their lines so well that they have virtually memorized them. Some students will want to add props or costumes, as the circumstances allow. More involved actors often begin to add accents to a character in the script.

Assessment

Base performance assessments on the pacing, volume, expression, and focus of the participants. Student-authored scripts should demonstrate general writing skills, dramatic tension, and a good plot. Class discussions should reflect serious thought, use of the background information, and references to the text of the script.

HAMMURABI'S LAW

BACKGROUND: HAMMURABI'S LAW

Babylon

The first city-states in history developed in Mesopotamia in the land between the Tigris and Euphrates rivers that flow into the Persian Gulf. There were many rulers and a great deal of conflict as various tribes tried to control the land that is today known as Iraq. Over many years, Babylon came to dominate the southern half of this area under a succession of rulers. In 1792 B.C. Hammurabi came to power in Babylon as the sixth ruler in a dynasty founded around 100 years before he became king.

Hammurabi

During the long reign of Hammurabi, from 1792 B.C. to 1750 B.C., the Babylonian empire was created as he defeated the many rivals for power from neighboring peoples. The peace he imposed led to successful years of bumper crops and increased trade among cities under his control. Merchants traveled to many lands trading grain and cloth for lumber, gold, gems, and livestock. The sciences, arts, medicine, poetry, literature, and education all flourished under his leadership. Mathematics developed with such inventions as square roots and cubic roots and a complex numbering system. Food was stored during years of plenty and used during years of drought and crop failure. Peace brought prosperity for many residents.

Hammurabi's Code of Laws

Toward the end of his rule, Hammurabi decided to issue a written code of laws, based on the customs and laws of his people, to which all citizens and residents would be able to refer. He had about 282 laws engraved on pillars in a temple in Babylon and available to be read by all. This is the first written code of laws in human history of which we have a record. The laws were designed to convey a sense of justice and equality based on social status and wealth.

The laws were remarkable in their detail and even protected the rights of women and slaves to a certain extent. Married Babylonian women even retained some control over their property and their persons. Slaves were permitted to earn wages after working for their owners, could own property, and buy their own freedom. Hammurabi's laws reflected the harsh realities of life in primitive nations, but they were the basis of future legal systems.

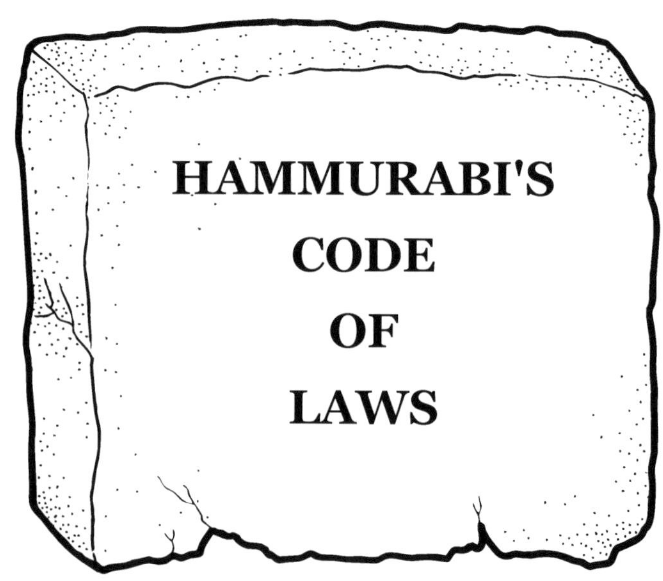

SCRIPT SUMMARY: HAMMURABI'S LAW

The setting for this script is a temple courtyard in Babylon a few years before 1750 B.C. The herald reads the laws of the kingdom that have been codified and inscribed on stone. The first law sets the tone for this ancient legal system that is an eye for an eye, a bone for a bone. If a pregnant woman is struck, loses the baby, and dies herself, the daughter of the person who struck the woman would be killed. Other punishments for serious crimes such as theft or murder, involve being thrown into a fire or being impaled (stabbed). The laws detail punishments involved for a wife embarrassing her husband, a son striking a father, and women entering a tavern.

The point of view of a merchant, a potter, a farmer, two wives, and a young man are expressed as various laws are read. The different status of free men and slaves is clear from the punishments. This is a society dependent upon slavery, and the speakers make clear their recognition of the dangers of slavery and their own fears of slave resistance. The narrator points out at the end of the script that Babylon was defeated by other nations soon after the death of Hammurabi.

Assignment

Read the readers' theater script "Hammurabi's Law." Prepare for the performances and share your interpretations of the scripts with the class.

Extensions: Writing and Literature

- Write a script based on Hammurabi's Laws. Use the background section, biographies, textbooks, and Internet sources for help. You can find a complete list of Hammurabi's laws on the Internet.

- Write a commentary or script of the laws from the viewpoint of a modern woman listening to the laws about women's rights and obligations.

- Write a commentary or script of the laws from the point of view of a slave (male or female) listening to the laws about the rights and obligations of slaves.

- Write a script rewriting the laws of Hammurabi from the viewpoint of today's life and culture.

- Imagine that you live in the time of Hammurabi. Create a script in which one of these laws plays a part in your life. You might be a citizen, a slave, a judge, a child, a farmer, a young married woman, or a thief.

- Read any biography of Hammurabi. Use one episode or a chapter as the basis for a readers' theater script about his life. After practicing your script, share your performance with the rest of the class.

SCRIPT: HAMMURABI'S LAW

This script is set in Babylon during the reign of Hammurabi from 1792 B.C. to 1750 B.C Hammurabi was a very competent king famous for having 282 basic laws of his kingdom carved into circular stone pillars. This script imagines the reading of the laws and reactions of various residents in the three classes of his kingdom: wealthy landowners and merchants, common workers and craftsmen, and slaves. There are eight speakers.

Narrator: Many people have crowded into a temple courtyard in central Babylon to hear the proclamation of the code of laws issued by Hammurabi. These laws are engraved on stone pillars to be read by the people. The laws are based on custom and tradition and are not new to the nation, but they were written so that all residents might have justice under law.

Herald: Hammurabi, the supreme leader in the world, has been instructed by the gods to make justice appear in the world and to destroy evil and the wicked so that the strong will not oppress the weak. His law will rise like the sun god to give light to the land.

Young Man: Our great leader is not a shy ruler, is he?

Herald: If a man put out the eye of another man, his eye shall be put out. If he breaks the bone of another man, his bone shall be broken. If he knocks out the teeth of his equal, his teeth shall be knocked out.

Merchant: That is perfectly fair and proper.

Herald: If a man strikes a free-born pregnant woman so that her child dies, he shall pay ten gold coins for her loss. If the woman dies, his daughter shall be put to death.

Potter's Wife: Notice that the women still lose.

Herald: A builder who sells a poorly constructed house that collapses and kills the buyer may be put to death. If the house collapses and kills the owner's son, the builder's son may be put to death.

Merchant: That ought to keep some of these dishonest builders from selling cheap death traps. The executions should be public to set an example for other builders.

SCRIPT: HAMMURABI'S LAW (cont.)

Herald: If a wife's bad behavior embarrasses her husband in public, he can be rid of her. If his claim is proven in court, he may divorce her and marry another woman. The first wife will then have the status of a household slave girl.

Merchant: Indeed, the women in this society are getting far too bossy and difficult. This should keep them in their place.

Potter: I will be sure to inform my wife of this new law. She complains as loudly as a fishwife. It's embarrassing, although she has been complaining and even worse, arguing, all of our married life.

Potter's Wife: What about his bad behavior—chasing slave girls or getting drunk?

Farmer's Wife: What good is a husband whose wife doesn't keep him in line?

Herald: If the wife of one man is unfaithful and arranges the murder of her husband and his wife, both the wife and the other man shall be impaled.

Potter: This is both fair and sensible. Otherwise, wives will be too tempted to seek the comfort of other men whenever their husbands ignore them.

Potter's Wife: Husbands could, of course, pay attention to their own wives and avoid the whole problem.

Herald: If an immoral woman opens a tavern or drinks in a tavern, this woman shall be burned to death. If a man's wife is accused of adultery but the charge is not proven, she shall jump into the river for her husband's honor.

Potter's Wife: Humph! I don't hear any law against men drinking or chasing other women.

Herald: If a son strikes his father, his hand may be cut off. If a slave strikes a free man, his ear may be cut off.

Young Man: You will notice that, according to this law, a son is little better than a slave.

SCRIPT: HAMMURABI'S LAW (cont.)

Herald: A man may leave property to his wife, but she may not sell the property. She must leave it to her sons.

Young Man: That is a very good law. It will keep a widow from wasting money on herself or getting married again.

Herald: A husband cannot divorce a sickly wife because of her illness. He is required to care for her in his home the rest of her life. But if a wife chooses to leave, she is free to leave and may take her dowry with her.

Farmer's Wife: That's at least fair to the wife.

Potter's Wife: It wouldn't have done me any good. My husband wasted my dowry the first year of our marriage on wine and gambling.

Herald: If a woman is disgraced in public by her husband and her accusations are proven in court, she can leave her husband and take her dowry.

Farmer's Wife: How are you going to prove you are disgraced in court without being even more embarrassed? I couldn't have lived on my meager dowry in any case.

Herald: If someone helps put out a fire and steals valuables from the burned building, the looter may be thrown into the fire.

Merchant: A very sensible and just ruling. Theft must always be punished.

Herald: If a farmer is unable to pay interest on a debt because of a crop failure or drought, the farmer may be excused from his debt that year.

Farmer: This is fair. Farming is a tough business, always dependent upon the weather and good luck.

Merchant: If you ask me, that just allows a farmer to squeeze out of his rightful debt. He should have to pay double interest next year.

Herald: If a slave strikes the body of a freeman, he shall receive 60 blows from an ox-whip in public.

Merchant: Slaves must be kept under control, or the whole country will fall to enemies in our own nation.

Herald: Someone who steals another person's slave, or hides a runaway slave intending to keep that slave as his own, may be put to death.

Potter: This will put an end to slave girls falling in love with young fools. They can both be properly punished.

Merchant: Indeed, you are right. Without slavery, our society would be much weaker. We would produce fewer goods and be less able to protect ourselves from enemies who would destroy Babylon and make us their slaves.

Farmer: But the slaves are here, and they hate us for our cruelty.

Merchant: Life is hard. Slavery is a reality of life. It is better to own slaves than to be slaves.

Potter: That is true, but life hangs on the threads of chance and the fickleness of the gods. It might not hurt to show kindness to the oppressed or at least treat the slave as a fellow human being.

Merchant: Kindness is weakness. Any enemy—any slave—will sense weakness, and then we will wear the brand and the yoke of slavery.

Herald: To the end of days, forever, may the king who happens to be in the land observe the words of justice that are inscribed here. The oppressed man shall read this writing, and he shall find his rights engraved in stone.

Narrator: The kingdom of Babylon barely survived the death of Hammurabi. Revolts within the kingdom were not defeated by his son, and invaders conquered the land. The stone pillars with the laws have survived as the first written account of an ancient people's code of laws governing all facets of life.

READER'S RESPONSE: HAMMURABI'S LAW

Directions

- These discussion activities and questions may be used in small groups or with the entire class. They may also be used by the actors as a part of their preparation for the reading.
- Refer to the script "Hammurabi's Law" when responding to all questions. Find useful facts in the background section, biographies, textbooks, and Internet sources.
- Make notes on the lines provided below each question before your group discussion.

General Discussion

1. Which of Hammurabi's laws was the most unfair? Explain your choice.

   ____

   ____

   ____

2. Which of Hammurabi's laws was the most reasonable? Why?

   ____

   ____

   ____

3. Why do you think the punishments were so severe in some cases?

   ____

   ____

   ____

4. What group or class of people were the most favored and protected by the code of laws? Explain your choice.

   ____

   ____

5. What group or class of people were least protected and least favored under the code of Hammurabi?

   ____

   ____

Making It Personal

How would you feel if you lived under the code of laws in Hammurabi's Babylon?

____

____

____

Slavery was very common in the ancient world. Why do you think it existed? Why have most societies and cultures eliminated slavery today?

____

____

READERS' THEATER

HER MAJESTY, HIMSELF

BACKGROUND: HER MAJESTY, HIMSELF

Egyptian Kingdoms

Egypt was settled by farmers as early as 6000 B.C. The first great era of power began with the Early Dynastic period about 3100 B.C. There were a series of kingdoms and royal dynasties until 1070 B.C. The New Kingdom was founded in 1550 B.C. Hatshepsut ruled as a pharaoh during this era. She came to power about 1498 B.C. and died about twenty years later.

The Reign of Hatshepsut

Hatshepsut was the daughter of Pharaoh Thutmosis I who recognized her intelligence and curiosity. She learned to read and write and was trained to be the wife of a future pharaoh. However, he also included her in some activities that were usually the preserve of boys, including hunting expeditions. Hatshepsut was trained to understand the importance of religious ceremonies and political rituals that were regarded as essential to maintaining Maat, a sense of order in the world.

Hatshepsut grew up in an era of prosperity. She was married in her early teens to her father's son by a member of his harem, Thutmosis II. (Arranged marriages between brothers and sisters were common for Egyptian royalty. It kept power consolidated in the family.) Thutmosis II was sickly and died a few years after becoming pharaoh.

Hatshepsut became the regent in charge of Egypt while Thutmosis III, her husband's son by another wife, was a child. Hatshepsut soon began to assume more responsibilities for running the two kingdoms of Egypt. She sent an expedition to the fabled kingdom of Punt which returned with many riches. She waged one brief, successful war with Nubia, and she built many monuments, temples, and statues. Hatshepsut had her tomb excavated within a mountain near the Valley of the Kings. She had a temple built for her at Deir El-Bahri near the Nile, not far from the capital at Thebes. It had a particularly beautiful and advanced style.

Hatshepsut gradually assumed the powers of a pharaoh and even wore a false beard as a sign of her power. She often had herself portrayed or referred to as a male. When Hatshepsut died, Thutmosis III finally assumed power as pharaoh. He had a very long and successful reign. He also tried to obliterate every sign of Hatshepsut's existence. Her name and features were carved out of stone monuments and statues. She was unknown until modern historians rediscovered her.

Script Summary: Her Majesty, Himself

The setting for this script is a palace courtyard where the future pharaoh, Thutmosis III, is talking to a general, an engineer, a scribe, and a priest, all of whom are members of Hatshepsut's inner circle of advisors. The discussion centers around the behavior and achievements of Queen Hatshepsut, the first Egyptian queen to assume the role of Pharaoh. There had never been a successful female ruler before her.

The characters describe the expedition sent to the fabled kingdom of Punt which returned with many luxurious items, including gold, ivory, exotic animals, and myrrh plants valued for their perfume. Her successful military action against Nubia is evaluated and much attention is paid to her many monuments, temples, and engravings which celebrate the queen's achievements. The scribe and engineer loyally describe her many successes. The general and priest are satisfied with the orderliness of her rule.

It is clear that Thutmosis III is angered by the power and decisions of the queen. He is also infuriated by her assumption of the male role of Pharaoh and her involvement in sacred ceremonies, sometimes dressed as a male. The narrator informs the audience that after her death, Pharaoh Thutmosis III tried, quite successfully, to eradicate every evidence of her existence.

Assignment

Read the readers' theater script "Her Majesty, Himself." Prepare for the performances and share your interpretations of the scripts with the class.

Extensions: Writing, Art, and Literature

- Write a script based on one of the events listed below or another one related to life in ancient Egypt. Use the background information section, biographies, textbooks, and Internet sources for help.

  The conflict between Akhenaten and the priests of Egypt

  The life of Ramses II

  Life of a craftsman, peasant, slave, or priest in ancient Egypt

  Getting a tomb ready for a pharaoh

  The life and death of Tutankhamen (King Tut)

- Use modeling clay, craft sticks, and other objects to recreate a sarcophagus, tomb, mummy, or pyramid. Be creative. Use books and pictures for models.
- Read the young adult novel, *His Majesty, Queen Hatshepsut* by Dorothy Sharp Carter. Use one episode or a chapter as the basis for a readers' theater script about the female pharaoh. Other good books include the humorous *Tut* by Jon Scieszka and the biography *Hatshepsut: His Majesty, Herself* by Catherine M. Andronik.

Script: Her Majesty, Himself

This script is set in a palace courtyard in Egypt about 1485 B.C. when Hatshepsut was the first successful queen of Egypt who ruled as a female pharaoh. There are six speakers.

Narrator: Ancient Egypt had been ruled from 3100 B.C. to 1500 B.C. by 18 dynasties or royal families. When there were no male heirs for a pharaoh, the Egyptian king, a relative or respected general took over as pharaoh and established his own dynasty. When Pharaoh Thutmosis I died, the new pharaoh was his son Thutmosis II, a sickly young man who was married to his half-sister, Hatshepsut. He soon died and she became the regent, the acting ruler, for Thutmosis III, her husband's baby son by another wife. Hatshepsut soon began to assume more and more power and control over the government of Egypt. This group of Egyptian court officials is talking with Thutmosis III, now in his twenties.

General: Her Highness, Pharaoh Hatshepsut, has accomplished another magnificent achievement, most honored Thutmosis. All of Thebes and the regions around our capital city are talking of the return of the expedition from the land of Punt.

Engineer: The ships we sent out two long years ago have returned filled to overflowing with the treasures of that fabled land. I did not truly believe that Punt existed. I thought it was an imaginary land dreamed up by the storytellers.

Scribe: You should see the wares the crew unloaded for Her Majesty. There were casks of perfumes and barrels of gold. Ivory and ebony were carried off in huge crates.

Thutmosis III: I suppose Her Majesty, the Pharaoh, my father's wife, was delighted with such things.

Priest: Yes, and the animals were truly remarkable. Panthers, leopards, spotted cats unknown to any of our people, giraffes, monkeys, and baboons were all placed in the royal zoo. There were even strange dark people from that land speaking a language no one knows.

SCRIPT: HER MAJESTY, HIMSELF (cont.)

Engineer: The most remarkable objects were myrrh trees. They were planted near Her Majesty's temple that she calls the "Holy of Holies." The special perfumes of these trees are very rare and, of course, especially valuable.

General: It must be admitted that Pharaoh Hatshepsut has been a remarkably successful ruler, for a woman.

Thutmosis III: No woman should rule Egypt. It has never been done before. Females don't have the intelligence or the courage to rule our double kingdom of Upper and Lower Egypt. They allow themselves to be influenced by others who are not even warriors or priests.

Scribe: I suppose that you are referring to me, most respected Son of a Pharaoh, but Hatshepsut was trained by your grandfather, her father, to do many things that only a pharaoh does. Maybe he saw the future and anticipated that she would one day rule Egypt. He observed that she could read and write as well as our most learned people. He trained her in all the intricacies of court behavior and dealing with foreign powers. He explained all of the mysteries of our gods and religious practices. He took her to many places when he traveled. He even took her crocodile hunting as a father does his son.

Thutmosis III: Girls in dresses shouldn't hunt crocodiles or wild cats either.

Engineer: I was there. Hatshepsut often dressed like a boy. She was as comfortable in a tunic as in a dress.

Priest: Girls should not wear boys' clothes. She wears that golden beard when she makes proclamations as Pharaoh. I worry that the Maat, the proper order of religion and life in Egypt, will be disturbed by her behavior. But the other priests support her, and life in Egypt under her leadership was been very peaceful and well ordered. The crops have been good every year, and the Nile River has favored us with fertile soil and water.

General: Her one military campaign against the Nubians was successful.

Thutmosis III: But she did not carry on the war until final victory. She accepted a quick victory. We might have subjugated the Nubians.

Scribe: Or, lost the entire war if it had gone badly.

Engineer: I am greatly impressed by her respect for the next life. She has carefully overseen every part of the construction of her burial chamber in the Valley of the Kings. Hatshepsut has even decided to bring her father's remains to her tomb where they will be safer from grave robbers and vandals.

Scribe: She has carefully hidden the location of her tomb. It will be safe from vandals. I have been fortunate enough to purchase a sarcophagus for myself near the tomb of Her Majesty. I hope to serve her in death as in life.

Thutmosis III: A lowly scribe does not deserve to be buried among the mighty.

Priest: You'd better be careful, or you will lose your place as a scribe at court as have others who have taken advantage of their positions. Hatshepsut wants no challengers to her power or authority.

Scribe: I have been her friend since childhood.

Thutmosis III: A true pharaoh does not have friends—only servants to obey his orders.

Engineer: One must admit that Hatshepsut does know how to celebrate. Her jubilee celebrating fifteen years as Pharaoh was magnificent. The two obelisks she had raised near her father's tomb at Karnak are among the greatest engineering achievements in all history. These golden-tipped tributes to the sun god, Re, were so tall that the rays of the sun reach them first before they strike the ground. They are the tallest structures ever built in Egypt. No one has ever seen such magnificent work.

Priest: Her monuments offer great praise to the gods of Egypt . . .

Thutmosis III: . . . and herself. They are made of stone. They will fall in time.

SCRIPT: HER MAJESTY, HIMSELF (cont.)

Priest: She always performs all of the religious and political ceremonies correctly.

Thutmosis III: Yes, but it is her daughter, Neferure, my chief wife, who acts as the wife of Pharaoh Hatshepsut in public ceremonies. It is disgraceful and embarrassing.

Priest: Well, it is a little unusual for a woman king to have her married daughter act as her wife, I suppose.

Engineer: Hatshepsut has constructed some of the greatest monuments in all of Egypt's history. Her splendid temple across the Nile from Karnak is built out of the mountain itself. It has taken many years.

Priest: The engravings on her temple offer praise to the gods.

Scribe: Her life story is told in the carvings on the wall so that everyone in the future will know of her power and the wonders of Egypt under her rule. The special design of the temple is mine, and she approved it. The story of her life has been engraved in stone on temples, palaces, and monuments here in Thebes and throughout Egypt for all of the ages to admire.

General: It is interesting that many of her engravings show Hatshepsut as a boy and others as a man. She is both male and female in the same stories carved into stone.

Thutmosis III: Even stone wears away. Vandals destroy many great buildings. Should people in the future even have to know that we had a female pharaoh? Maybe her successor will be so great that she will disappear like dust in the wind.

Narrator: Hatshepsut died in her forties after nineteen years in power, possibly of natural causes and possibly from poison or murder. She was succeeded by Thutmosis III who had a long and successful rule. During his years as pharaoh, he had Hatshepsut's name and engravings defaced and destroyed in many places. Her tomb was hidden from view. Stonecutters chopped away her face from hundreds of statues. Her name was removed from many stone inscriptions. Thutmosis tried to eradicate any sign of her rule or existence. Even her mummified body is missing.

Reader's Response: Her Majesty, Himself

Directions

- These discussion activities and questions may be used in small groups or with the entire class. They may also be used by the actors as a part of their preparation for the reading.
- Refer to the script "Her Majesty, Himself" when responding to all questions. You may also find useful facts in the background information section, biographies, textbooks, and Internet sources.
- Make notes on the lines provided below each question before the group discussion.

Discussion

1. Why do you think Thutmosis disliked Queen Hatshepsut? Give several reasons.

2. Which of the characters in the script is most supportive of Hatshepsut as Pharaoh? Explain your choice.

3. Who do you think the priest and the general would support in a conflict between Hatshepsut and Thutmosis? Explain your choice.

4. What is your opinion of life (and death) in ancient Egypt?

Making It Personal

Would you like to have been an Egyptian pharaoh? Why?

Do you admire what Hatshepsut accomplished or do you support the attitude of Thutmosis? Explain your choice.

Thutmosis says the pharaoh should have no friends—only servants. What do you think of his comment?

READERS' THEATER
THE COURAGE
OF A QUEEN

BACKGROUND: THE COURAGE OF A QUEEN

Ancient Israel

About 1700 B.C., a tribe of people called the Hebrews migrated from Ur in Mesopotamia to the land of Palestine at the eastern edge of the Mediterranean Sea. The Hebrews engaged in warfare with the tribes who were already there and over time formed the nation of Israel with its capital, Jerusalem. Israel had several periods of prosperity and decline.

Because of its crucial location along trade routes from Egypt to Asia, it was often subject to attack from its more powerful neighbors. Assyria conquered the northern kingdom in 721 B.C. and took thousands of Jews to Assyria. In 597 B.C., the Babylonian king Nebuchadnezzar conquered Jerusalem and deported many Jews from the southern kingdom of Judah to Babylon.

Jews lived for decades under Babylonian and Persian rule before King Cyrus the Great allowed them to return to their homeland. Many others stayed because they had land, good jobs, or foreign wives and families. These are the Jews living in the Persian empire during the reign of Xerxes.

Esther

The story of Esther is set in Persia during the reign of Xerxes I. The time is about 480 B.C., more than 100 years after the Babylonian captivity of the Jews. Esther is a Jewish girl who becomes a queen of Persia and saves her people from genocide. Whether the story is historically accurate is uncertain, but it does reflect the constant conflicts and invasions between the small nation states of Israel and its many warlike neighbors over a period of centuries. It also illustrates the cultural and religious differences between Jews and other peoples.

According to the story that is recorded in the Hebrew bible, Esther was chosen to be queen of Persia by King Xerxes after the previous queen had been banished for a minor act of disobedience to the king. Esther adopts a Persian name and does not tell the king of her heritage. Haman, an arrogant and self-absorbed prime minister, expected all officials to bow to him, but Esther's cousin, Mordecai, as a Jew refuses to bow before any man. Haman dupes the rather distracted king into ordering the destruction of all Jews in the Persian Empire. According to the story, Esther bravely faces the anger of the king for her own disobedience and intercedes with King Xerxes to save her people.

SCRIPT SUMMARY: THE COURAGE OF A QUEEN

The setting for this script is the capital city of Susa in the Persian Empire ruled by Xerxes I in about 480 B.C. Many thousands of Jews are living in the empire. The rather unpredictable and light-minded king banishes Queen Vashti for not leaving a banquet she is hosting so that he can show off her beauty before the assembled notables at his banquet. The king orders a search through all of his kingdoms for the most beautiful woman in Persia to become his new queen.

Mordecai, a respected judge who is a Jew, recognizes that his cousin, Hadassah, is so beautiful that she is going to be among the women ordered to the palace. Mordecai tells Hadassah to adopt the Persian name, Esther, and avoid any mention of her Jewish heritage, because some people would hold it against her. Esther is eventually chosen as queen because of her simplicity, beauty, and humor.

Mordecai earns the anger of the new Prime Minister, Haman, because, as a practicing Jew, he refuses to bow before anyone but God. Haman determines to take revenge by duping the king into approving the destruction of all the Jews in the empire. Esther disobeys the orders of the king, tells him of her Jewish heritage, and offers to give up her position and her life. Xerxes countermands the order, has Haman hung on his own gallows, and the Jews are saved from destruction.

Assignment

Read the readers' theater script "The Courage of a Queen." Prepare for the performance and share your interpretations of the scripts with the class.

Extensions: Writing and Literature

- Write a script based on one of the events listed below or another one related to the history of the nation of Israel. Use the background information section, biographies, textbooks, and Internet sources for help.

  David becomes King of Israel.

  David fights the Philistines.

  Joshua leads the Hebrew army into Palestine and attacks Jericho.

  Deborah leads a Hebrew army against the Canaanites.

  Judith wages war against the Assyrian army.

- Read any version of the Old Testament in the Bible. Use one story or episode as the framework for a readers' theater script based on the events or people of ancient Israel. After practicing your script, share your performance with the rest of the class.

This script is set in Persia during the reign of Xerxes I. The time is about 480 B.C. Many Jews lived freely in the Persian Empire and some held important positions in business and government. This story of a Jewish girl who becomes Queen of Persia and saves her people from genocide is of uncertain historical origins, but it reflects the real conflicts between the people of Israel and their powerful neighbors. There are six speakers.

Narrator: King Xerxes prepared a huge banquet at his palace in the capital city of Susa. He invited all of his important ministers. The celebrations went on for seven nights and included a great deal of drinking and feasting. A prominent judge named Mordecai, a Jewish resident of the city, attended the banquet. Mordecai is respected for his wisdom and his learning. He speaks several languages in this empire of many peoples and cultures.

King Xerxes: Where is Vashti, my Queen, the most beautiful woman in all of my kingdom? Send for her now. I want all of my guests to see the most beautiful woman in the world.

Hegai: Queen Vashti is hosting a banquet for the great ladies of the kingdom.

King Xerxes: Let them feast without her. Send for my beautiful queen now.

Haman: Your majesty, Vashti, the Queen of all Persia, refuses to leave the banquet she is hosting. She has defied your command.

King Xerxes: This insult is unendurable. I will not be ignored. I will not suffer the disobedience and disrespect of any woman.

Haman: Indeed, it will set a terrible example for all the women of the empire. A woman's obedience must be total and immediate. Such defiance must be punished now.

SCRIPT: THE COURAGE OF A QUEEN (cont.)

King Xerxes: So it will be. Banish Vashti from the palace immediately. Remove her crown. Take away all of her rich clothes and precious jewels. Vashti is no longer the queen of all my domains. Send her into the streets to beg for her food.

Hegai: But, Sire, what shall you do for a queen? The queen must provide heirs for your majesty.

King Xerxes: Send this message to all of the 127 provinces of Persia. Let the governors of the farthest of my domains be notified. The king will choose a new queen from among the most beautiful women of Persia. All of these women are summoned to my palace to be inspected by my officials. I shall choose the most beautiful young woman for my queen.

Narrator: Mordecai went home from the banquet after Queen Vashti's banishment with a heavy heart. He knew that the king was often quick-tempered in his actions and not very sensible in his judgments. He also knew that his cousin Hadassah, an orphan who lived in his home, was known to be the most beautiful girl in the city. The king had already sent messengers ordering every beautiful woman to be summoned to his palace. When he went home, he talked to his cousin.

Mordecai: Hadassah, my beloved cousin, Queen Vashti has been banished for her disobedience to King Xerxes. All of the beautiful women of Persia have been summoned for inspection by the king's servants. He will choose a new queen from among these women. You must change your Jewish name and take the Persian name Esther, because you are as beautiful as Esther, the morning and evening star. You must not tell the attendants at court that you are Jewish. Some will want to harm you because of your race and our different customs and beliefs.

SCRIPT: THE COURAGE OF A QUEEN (cont.)

Esther: I will do as you say, Mordecai, but no king will choose me. I do not wish to be a queen, and others will be far more beautiful.

Mordecai: I fear for you, Esther, but you must be strong.

Narrator: Esther spent several months living with the other young women who had been summoned. She made many friends because of her kindness and modesty. Each night one woman was dressed in rich clothes, decorated with expensive jewelry, and carefully made up to enhance her beauty. Every young woman was rejected by the king. He became more irritated and difficult with each passing week. Several months after her arrival, Esther was summoned by the servants to meet King Xerxes. She refused all of the fine fabrics and insisted on wearing a simple white dress. She wore no jewelry or makeup and only a single rose in her long black hair. She went to meet the king by walking through the seven hallways that led to his residence, a passageway no one could use without permission.

King Xerxes: Truly, you are a vision from the gods. What is your name?

Esther: I am called Esther for the morning star.

Narrator: The king stood with his arms folded. Esther folded her arms and faced him. A rose petal fell from her hair. The king picked it up and put it on her cheek. She took it and placed it in a curl of his hair.

Esther: How beautiful you are, Your Majesty. You should wear roses, too.

King Xerxes: No star in all the heavens shines with your perfect beauty. You are the most beautiful woman in all the world. You shall be my queen. Wear this crown as your own.

SCRIPT: THE COURAGE OF A QUEEN (cont.)

Narrator: Not long after the wedding, Mordecai was walking through the hallways of the palace on business and hoping to see his cousin when he overheard two servants plotting to assassinate the king with poisonous food. Mordecai sent a message to Esther telling her of the plot, so she could warn the king. Esther warned Xerxes, and the plot was foiled. Mordecai's warning was recorded in the king's diary that was often read to him at night. At this time, Haman became the new Prime Minister of the empire. He was very arrogant and expected all of the other ministers, judges, and servants to bow down before him, which was a common Persian custom. Haman was walking by Mordecai in the courtyard one day when he passed Mordecai who refused to bow his head.

Haman: You! What is your name? Why do you not bow your head in respect as all others do?

Mordecai: Prime Minister, I am a Jew. I bow to no man.

Haman: This is outrageous. I will have none of this. Next time we meet, you must bow. Do you hear me?

Mordecai: I hear your words, but I will not break faith with my people. We bow only to our God.

Narrator: Several times they met and each time Mordecai refused to bow his head to the ground. Finally, Haman met with the king who was occupied playing a card game with several officials. As usual, he did not wish to be bothered with any business of the kingdom.

Haman: Sire, there are many people of the Jewish race scattered throughout our great empire. They set themselves apart from all others and refuse to obey our laws and customs. The disrespect of the Jews can no longer be tolerated. They must be killed to the last person—men, women, and children alike.

SCRIPT: THE COURAGE OF A QUEEN (cont.)

King Xerxes: Fine. You may do whatever you desire. I'm busy at the moment.

Narrator: Haman went home and rolled dice to determine the best date for the destruction of all the Jews in the Persian Empire. The date rolled was several months in the future. He also had a scaffold made for the hanging of Mordecai whose refusal to bow he considered both an insult and an embarrassment. The Jews were soon informed of the death sentence, and many tried to flee. Others went into mourning and prayed for deliverance. Mordecai sent a message to Esther asking her to intercede with the king, even though she was never permitted to interrupt the king or seek his company without his consent. If she did try to see him, it would be an act of disobedience punishable by banishment. Esther spent three days in deep praying and fasting. Then she disobeyed the rules and walked through the seven hallways that led to the king's quarters.

King Xerxes: Esther, why do you enter my quarters? You have not been summoned. But you are truly as beautiful as the morning star. Whatever you wish is yours, even if it is half of my kingdom. I can deny you nothing.

Esther: Your Supreme Majesty, my wish is not for myself but for my people. You have issued an order that all of the people of my race, the Jews, are to be killed. I have been informed of this by my cousin Mordecai, the judge, the same person who warned you of an assassination attempt. Banish me if you wish. Kill me if you must, but save my people who are both innocent and loyal.

King Xerxes: Who has issued such a despicable order?

Esther: Your Prime Minister, Haman, used your signet ring to order all of the Jews in the realm to be killed in the thirteenth day of the twelfth month.

SCRIPT: THE COURAGE OF A QUEENr *(cont.)*

Haman: This person is only a woman and not even a Persian princess at that. For her disobedience, she should be banished or killed.

Narrator: Haman moved toward Esther with his fist raised, but Esther stood her ground ready to be beaten.

King Xerxes: No one will slay my Esther or the Jews in my kingdom. Guards! Seize Haman. I hear that he has erected a scaffold near his house. Let him hang from his own noose. Let him die on his own gallows. Esther, summon your cousin, Mordecai.

Narrator: Esther left and soon returned with Mordecai, who had waited in the courtyard.

King Xerxes: Mordecai, loyal servant of the king, you will be the new Prime Minister. Send messages by the fastest horses throughout my kingdoms. No Jews are to be killed. Those Jews who are attacked may defend themselves even against the soldiers of the empire.

Narrator: The sons of Haman were powerful, and some of the governors did not obey their king's orders. Many street battles were fought across the empire. Even in the capital of Susa, the battles went on for days, but in the end, the Jews survived the attacks and continued to live in the empire and serve its kings until it was destroyed by other conquering warlords.

READER'S RESPONSE: THE COURAGE OF A QUEEN

Directions

- These discussion activities and questions may be used in small groups or with the entire class. They may also be used by the actors as a part of their preparation for the reading.
- Refer to the script "The Courage of a Queen" when responding to all questions. You may also find useful facts in the background information section, biographies, textbooks, and Internet sources.
- Make notes on the lines provided below each question before your group discussion.

General Discussion

1. Which of the characters did you like best? Explain your choice.

____

____

____

2. Compare some of the cultural, legal, and social behaviors and attitudes of ancient Persia with the United States today.

____

____

____

3. Why do you think Haman was so irritated by Mordecai's refusal to bow?

____

____

Making It Personal

What is your opinion of Xerxes as a person and a king? Do you think there are men like Xerxes today?

____

____

____

Would you like to be chosen as a queen or king based on your beauty alone? Explain your answer.

____

____

____

Should Mordecai have been willing to bow to Haman as other officials did? Explain your response.

____

____

____

Why do you think Esther won the king's heart?

____

____

READERS' THEATER

THE TRIAL OF SOCRATES

BACKGROUND: THE TRIAL OF SOCRATES

Athens

Athens was a Greek city-state that had once been ruled by a few powerful aristocratic leaders and sometimes by tyrants. In about the year 500 B.C., Athenians created a democracy based on the idea of citizenship. Although the number of citizens was limited, Athens became the first democracy in the Mediterranean world. This form of government lasted about 170 years from 500 B.C. to about 330 B.C.

Citizenship was limited to free men who owned property. Women, slaves, foreigners, and men without property were not citizens. Modern ideas of democracy, including the rule of law, majority rule, and the idea of government run by the people, developed in this ancient Greek city. In the time of Socrates, Athens was a city of about 400,000 people, but about 250,000 were slaves. Athens had been a great power in Greece, with a great deal of wealth, a powerful navy, and a successful army. Athens was eventually defeated by other city-states led by Sparta in 404 B.C. This Peloponnesian War lasted 27 years, and Athens never regained its former power or influence.

Socrates

Socrates was a short, squat, powerful man who had served many years in the Athenian army in his youth where he was regarded as a brave and competent soldier. His father had been a working man, and Socrates inherited a small house and some property. He was born about ten years after the Greek defeat of the Persians in 480 B.C. Socrates lived through most of Athens' glory years and then the ultimate defeat by Sparta.

Socrates was one of the most famous citizens of Athens. He was known for his learning and was regarded as a great teacher and philosopher. He was also an eccentric thinker, and his ideas were sometimes regarded as dangerous to Athens. He challenged conventional beliefs about Greek religion, and he distrusted the motivations and behavior of its elected officials. Socrates had a rocky relationship with his unhappy wife who was often loud and angry because he didn't earn an income. Socrates was brought to trial before a group of 501 citizen judges on charges of disrespect for the Greek gods and corrupting the minds of the young. He was convicted and refused to ask for exile. Instead, he drank a cup of hemlock poison and died. Many of Socrates' teachings were later recorded by his student, Plato.

SCRIPT SUMMARY: THE TRIAL OF SOCRATES

The setting for this script is Athens, Greece in the year 399 B.C. Officials in the city have charged the philosopher Socrates with disrespect toward the Greek gods who are part of the religious and social heritage of the city. He has also been accused of corrupting the youth of the city by encouraging them to question authority and accepted beliefs. Socrates is to be judged by 501 citizens of Athens who will determine by majority vote if he is guilty. He is questioned about his opinions and statements. Socrates admits that he is a seeker of truth and wisdom and that he does not believe in the Greek gods of Mount Olympus. He does believe in a universal God, and he follows an inner voice in determining what is right and wrong.

Socrates also expresses his distrust for the motivation and behavior of the city's leaders. Members of the court point out that he spends most of each day talking with people and asking questions, a behavior that irritates his wife, as well as the city fathers. Socrates is found guilty of the charges, and he refuses to accept exile rather than the death penalty. He intends to follow the law even when it is a bad law, because he believes in the rule of law. He drinks a cup of poison hemlock and dies. His student, Plato, says that Socrates was the most honorable and intelligent man he has ever known.

Assignment

Read the readers' theater script "The Trial of Socrates." Prepare for the performances and share your interpretations of the scripts with the class.

Extensions: Writing, Literature, and Art

- Write a script based on one of the events listed below or another one related to Socrates, ancient Athens, or the ancient Greek thinkers. Use the background information section, biographies, textbooks, and Internet sources for help.

  Socrates talks with his students and citizens on his daily rounds.

  Socrates and his wife argue about his lack of income and "lazy" behavior.

  Plato and Socrates discuss the meaning of life.

- Read the *Iliad* or the *Odyssey*, long narrative poems by Homer. Choose a small section of one of the stories to create a readers' theater script. You might also choose one of Aesop's fables.

- Create a model of the city of Athens in ancient times with many of its public monuments, temples, and important buildings. Use construction paper, tagboard, and other materials to show as many details as possible. Include Socrates and citizens in the display.

Script: The Trial of Socrates

This script is set in ancient Athens in the year 399 B.C. There are seven speakers.

Narrator: Socrates was one of the most famous citizens of Athens, a once-powerful Greek city-state that had been defeated by its enemies. Socrates had been a brave and competent soldier in his youth. He owned a small home and inheritance and did not work for a living. He spent most of his adult life wandering the streets discussing politics, the meaning of life, religion, philosophy, and current events. He upset the political leaders and public officials of Athens because many of the questions he asked either made fun of them or challenged their decisions. He has been brought to trial before a group of 501 citizens who will serve as his judges and determine his fate.

Meletus: Socrates, citizen of Athens, you are brought to trial before 501 of your fellow citizens serving as your judges. The charges against you are these. First, you are accused of believing in gods other than the Greek deities who have protected Athens throughout our history. Secondly, you are charged with corrupting the young people of Athens with your ideas. Do you understand the charges?

Socrates: I understand the charges, but not why I have been charged.

Meletus: Is it not true that you have often criticized the actions of the government and the leaders of Athens? You constantly speak to all manner of citizens, residents, and even slaves about the issues of the day, and you are extremely critical. You disparage the motives of the leaders of our great city. How do you plead?

Socrates: I was a soldier throughout the wars of my youth when Athens fought Sparta and the other Greek city-states allied against us. Our failure to win was partly due to the self-interest of our leaders and the lack of military skill of those men. Many of the officials of Athens look to their own interests rather than to the welfare of all. They desire reelection, extra profits for their businesses, more slaves, and warfare with our neighbors.

SCRIPT: THE TRIAL OF SOCRATES *(cont.)*

Anytus: You all heard his words. He is still demeaning the great men who run our city.

Plato: *(aside)* Of course, Anytus and Meletus both consider themselves part of the brilliant corps of leaders who claim to represent the people.

Lycon: I have heard you insult the gods of Greece on any number of occasions. We have been defeated by our enemies because of the impiety and disbelief of you and your followers. You have encouraged the young men of this city to distrust and be disrespectful of the gods. Do you deny that you follow another god?

Socrates: I do not disrespect any god, but I don't believe in the gods said to be residing on Mount Olympus. They do not even agree with each other on most things, if you listen to the priests. I do believe in one powerful god of the universe. I follow a voice within myself that helps me determine right from wrong. I trust my inner voice more than any god.

Lycon: You can hear the blasphemy with your own ears. How does a man hear voices unless he has drunk too much wine?

Chaerephon: Even the oracle at Delphi who is in touch with the gods told me there was no man wiser than Socrates. Are you the wisest man of all?

Socrates: I don't believe the oracle. I am not a wise person. I just love wisdom. I know nothing compared to the whole of what can be learned. I seek wisdom from every person I meet. I am a philosopher. The meaning of philosophy is to love knowledge, and knowledge leads to wisdom—sometimes. We should immediately go in search of a man more intelligent than I to prove the gods are wrong.

Meletus: His very words insult the gods.

SCRIPT: THE TRIAL OF SOCRATES (cont.)

Plato: My teacher, Socrates, believes that the only way to find truth is to believe you know nothing. This is not an insult to the gods. It is simple humility. He is the most intelligent man I have ever known.

Anytus: Socrates, do you wish to throw yourself on the mercy of these judges and possibly save your own life?

Socrates: If I wished to seek mercy, I would have brought my wife and children to beg for me. I did not choose to do so.

Chaerephon: It's a good thing he didn't bring his wife. She is forever nagging and screaming at the poor man in her loud, thundering voice. One time she set a jug of water over the door, and it fell on his head. Of course, Socrates made a joke of it. He said it always rains after it thunders.

Meletus: You have also been accused of disrespect toward Athens. Are you a true citizen of Athens?

Socrates: I am not just a citizen of Athens or even of Greece. I am a citizen of the world.

Lycon: That is nonsense. No one is a citizen of the world. You must either be with us or against us.

Anytus: You ignore your wife and do no work. Everyone has heard the loud and continuous complaints of your wife.

Socrates: This is true. If you marry a good woman, your life will be filled with joy. If you marry a nagging woman, you may become a philosopher.

SCRIPT: THE TRIAL OF SOCRATES (cont.)

Lycon: You can be found daily wandering the streets, talking to people, especially idle youths. Your endless questions disturb the peace of their unsettled minds. These questions are discussed by many citizens and sow dissension among the people. You challenge the very political system you live under. Your remarks will stir up insurrection and revolt among slaves and people without property. You have offended most of the powerful people of Athens with your endless questions.

Socrates: If I do not question, I cannot learn. My purpose in life is to seek what I do not know and spread what I do know to others. Don't you—all of you—feel ashamed at what you do not know? The very soul of man seeks knowledge.

Meletus: We have heard enough of this man's testimony. His own words condemn him. Let the judges be counted.

Narrator: A total of 281 of the 501 citizens who were judges in the trial of Socrates voted for his guilt on the charge of disrespect for the gods. The punishment was death, but often exile from the city was offered instead.

Meletus: Do you wish to ask for exile from Athens instead of the death sentence that has been handed down?

Socrates: No. I believe in the law, even when it is wrong. The law is not perfect, but it must guide the way I live. Today you may judge me, but in the future, history will judge you.

Plato: It is my good fortune to have been born in Socrates' lifetime and to have been his student. He is the most honorable man in all of Athens.

Narrator: Socrates was allowed to drink a cup of hemlock, a deadly poison. He died peacefully, believing that death would free his spirit.

READER'S RESPONSE: THE TRIAL OF SOCRATES

Directions

- These discussion activities and questions may be used in small groups or with the entire class. They may also be used by the actors as a part of their preparation for the reading.
- Refer to the script "The Trial of Socrates" when responding to all questions. You may also find useful facts in the background section, biographies, textbooks, and Internet sources.
- Make notes on the lines provided below each question before your group discussion.

General Discussion

1. How does democracy in Athens differ from democracy in your country?

____

____

____

2. What do you think of Socrates' answers to the charges of not being faithful to the Greek gods? What did he believe in?

____

____

____

3. Why do you think Socrates angered the officials in Athens so much?

____

____

____

4. Do you think Socrates' wife had good reasons for nagging him? How would you feel if you were Socrates or his wife?

____

____

____

Making It Personal

Do you think Socrates made the correct decision in refusing exile? What would you have done in this situation? Explain your answers.

____

____

____

Would you like to be a person like Socrates in today's world? How would you have to change to follow his ideas about truth and wisdom?

____

____

____

READERS' THEATER
ALEXANDER'S
MUTINY

BACKGROUND: ALEXANDER'S MUTINY

Alexander the Great

Alexander the Great was born in 356 B.C. in Macedonia, the son of King Philip II. Macedonians spoke a Greek dialect and considered themselves Greek but were considered barbarians by Athenians and other Greek city states because they were ruled by kings. In his teens, Alexander was tutored by Aristotle, the most famous Greek philosopher of his time. Alexander tamed a wild horse named Bucephalus in his youth and rode the horse for over twenty years. Alexander spent his teen years learning the military arts.

When he was 20, Alexander's father, King Philip, was murdered and the army chose Alexander as his successor. He immediately went to war against the Greek cities that revolted when Philip died. He defeated Thebes and brought all of Greece under his control. He then began a long campaign against the Persian Empire ruled by King Darius. Alexander had an army of more than 37,000 soldiers, including about 5,000 mounted horse soldiers. His army traveled with many wives and women camp followers as well as surveyors, engineers, astronomers, priests of various religions, a secretary, and an historian.

Alexander defeated Persian armies at Issus in what is now Turkey, and later captured the well-protected city of Tyre, which severely weakened the Persian navy. Alexander then traveled to Egypt, which had belonged to Persia. He was crowned pharaoh by the Egyptians—they were grateful to get rid of their Persian overlords. Alexander founded the famous city of Alexandria in Egypt and returned to Persia to defeat Darius again. He captured Babylonia, Susa, Persepolis, and other great cities as part of his victory. Alexander captured over 7,000 tons of treasure and used it to finance all of his future battles. He later defeated Darius' successor, Bessus, and traveled through what is now Afghanistan to the Hindu Kush Mountains which were the gateway to India.

After defeating King Porus in northern India, Alexander's army mutinied and insisted on going home. Alexander finally agreed but took a very rough and dangerous route home along the Indus River to the Indian Ocean. Alexander was wounded in a battle and later died of malaria on his way back to Babylon in 323 B.C., at the age of 32. A bitter power struggle arose after his death among his generals and supporters of his wife and infant son. All of his relatives were murdered in the conflict and his empire was divided up by his generals.

Script Summary: Alexander's Mutiny

The setting for this script is about 325 B.C. in northern India. Alexander the Great wants to continue his campaign of conquest and capture of India, which he thinks is a small land on the edge of Asia. His men want to go home after ten years of fighting. Coenus is their spokesman but others also complain. The Macedonian soldiers resent that he is putting on airs like a Persian king, a Greek god, or an Egyptian pharaoh. He has become a god in his own mind. They also complain about his acceptance of Persian customs and culture. Alexander killed two of his closest friends in a drunken rage which also disturbs the men.

Alexander's closest friend, Hephaistion, defends the war leader, but Craterus and others complain about India—the snakes, crocodiles, fevers, insects, skin sores, polluted water, wretched food, and difficult mountains. Coenus, speaking for the men, says they refuse to go farther. Alexander threatens to go on alone or with a new army of Persian soldiers. He offers to give the men Persian wives, but nothing sways their determination to go home. Alexander ultimately agrees but insists on going by a new route with a divided army. He is wounded and dies on the way home.

Assignment

Read the readers' theater script "Alexander's Mutiny." Prepare for the performances and share your interpretations of the scripts with the class.

Extensions: Writing, Literature, and Art

- Write a script based on one of events listed below or another one related to Alexander the Great. Use the background section, biographies, textbooks, and Internet sources for help.

  As a young teen, Alexander tames Bucephalus, who becomes his special warhorse.

  In his youth, Alexander and his famous tutor, Aristotle, discuss the meaning of life.

  Alexander defeats Darius, the Persian king, and captures his empire.

  Alexander goes to Egypt, founds Alexandria, and becomes a pharaoh.

  The death of Alexander the Great

- Read any biography of Alexander the Great. Use one episode or a chapter as the basis for a readers' theater script about Alexander's life. After practicing your script, share your performance with the rest of the class.

- Use modeling clay or artist's clay to mold a bust of Alexander the Great, his horse, or one of his wives. You might choose to do a portrait with colored pencils or markers of the same subjects.

SCRIPT: ALEXANDER'S MUTINY

This script is set in India in 326 B.C. after Alexander the Great's Macedonian army had defeated an Indian army led by King Porus. Alexander wants to invade the rest of India. His men want to go home and refuse to go any farther. The script explains the reasons for their mutiny. There are eight speakers.

Narrator: The army of Alexander the Great has fought for ten years across more than 22,000 miles from Macedonia and Greece in the eastern Mediterranean Sea through the Persian Empire in the Middle East and Egypt and on into northern India. Alexander believes that India is a small land at the edge of Asia, and he wants to conquer that land next. His men want to go home. They mutiny. They refuse to cross one more river on the way into India. The men hold a meeting to present their grievances to Alexander.

Coenus: The time, Alexander, has come to go home. We are your most loyal soldiers, but the time has come to return to our wives and children. The one thing a successful general should know is when to stop.

Alexander: Soldiers of Macedon, we have conquered every nation we have encountered. We have never been defeated in battle. India awaits with all of its wealth. There will be riches beyond anything you can imagine. The land is filled with rubies and sapphires and other precious gems. Look at the wealth we won in Persia. Remember how just and generous I have been in sharing the spoils of war. All of you have gained gold and silver, precious gems, and the finest treasure from the lands of Persia, Egypt, and India.

Coenus: That is true, Alexander, but we cannot spend our wealth from the grave. We have been gone so long our wives will have given us up for dead, and our sons would not even recognize us. Our parents will be old or dead.

SCRIPT: ALEXANDER'S MUTINY (cont.)

Demaratus: Even worse, our wives will have grown old and lonely. They may have found new husbands who are there while we are here.

Hegelochus: The gods have supported us so far, but it is not wise to tempt their anger. We have conquered most of the world. It is not wise to be so greedy.

Coenus: Alexander, you think of yourself as a god. You have become too Persian. You act like the kings of Persia who allowed people to worship them. It is not right for a soldier of Macedonia to permit even worthless Persians to blow kisses at you and prostrate themselves on the ground with their heads touching the earth. It is not proper behavior for a warrior chosen king by the soldiers of the Macedonian army.

Hegelochus: You have even claimed to be the son of Zeus, the king of the gods of Greece. It is not right to tempt the anger of the gods. In Egypt, you let them crown you as a pharaoh, a god-king. Next thing, you will want them to build a great pyramid for you like those ancient tombs.

Narrator: The men discuss their complaints among themselves as Alexander tries to find words that will change their minds.

Demaratus: Alexander has already given orders that his body is to be mummified. A pyramid will be next.

Hegelochus: It isn't any worse than acting Persian. He associates with Persian princes now. He walks among the Persian soldiers and dresses like a Persian king. That is no way for a good Macedonian warrior to behave. He has as many Persian friends as Greek warriors.

Script: Alexander's Mutiny (cont.)

Craterus: Indeed, we are an army of Macedonians and Greeks, not the barbarian sons of conquered foreigners. It is another sign of Alexander's misguided actions. We conquered all Persia, but Persian culture has conquered us.

Demaratus: Alexander has lost his mind, I think. Look what happened to Philotas, his friend and a great general. Philotas complained as we are doing about our endless journey. Alexander decided he was a traitor and had him tortured and killed.

Hegelochus: Even worse, Cleitus was a valiant war leader who dared to criticize Alexander in public. Alexander grabbed a spear and stabbed his friend Cleitus to death. Cleitus had saved his life in the battle at Granicus River. Alexander has shown no loyalty to the men who loyally followed him. He had General Parmenio killed, too.

Coenus: Victory has affected his judgment, but defeat might make him even more stubborn.

Nearchus: He has become a god to himself. He has named seventeen cities Alexandria, after himself. Now he has named a city in honor of his horse, Bucephalus.

Hephaistion: Alexander is still the greatest war leader of all time. He has led us for ten years. We have never been defeated and never retreated without ultimate victory. We have destroyed armies three and four times as large as our own. We have been paid for years with the treasure of the defeated Persian kings. Alexander has always been generous with us. We soldiers are his family.

SCRIPT: ALEXANDER'S MUTINY (cont.)

Demaratus: You are Alexander's closest boyhood friend and defend him well, but the battles have worn us out. We have fought for over ten years, and we suffered thousands of lives lost in defeating King Darius and chasing his successor, Bessus, all over the Persian Empire. His decisions do not make sense. We just defeated King Porus, and Alexander made him a more powerful king than he was.

Narrator: Alexander has heard enough. He wants to cross the river into the rest of India and tries to convince his troops once again to trust him.

Alexander: I made Porus a king because he fought bravely and did not run away like that coward Darius did. This king's courage will make him a good ally in the battles against the rest of India.

Coenus: Or, it will allow Porus to build up another army. No barbarian from India, Persia, or Egypt can ever be trusted. We are Macedonians and Greeks. We must trust ourselves.

Craterus: We are tired of India. We did not come here to sleep with snakes and swim with crocodiles at every river crossing. The elephants used in this land stink, and they upset our horses. We were very lucky to destroy those 200 elephants in the last battle. They might have led to our defeat.

Alexander: We have conquered every army we ever faced. When will a few elephants defeat an army of Macedon? I who built a navy and conquered invincible Tyre. I who cut the Gordian Knot with a slash of my sword. Do you no longer trust me?

Craterus: I have crossed enough mountains. Those mountain passes in the Hindu Kush leading to India were terrible to both men and horses.

SCRIPT: ALEXANDER'S MUTINY (cont.)

Nearchus: And what did we find? Endless rain, soaking heat that rots our skin, and insects like all of the devils in Hades itself. Hundreds have been bitten by snakes. We have more sores than skin. The food is wretched and what there is of it is spoiled. It is worse than the stinking food in the rocky deserts we crossed to get to the mountains. The drinking water is polluted and makes most of the army sick. This land is not worth owning. It is a waste of effort to destroy armies protecting such a worthless place. The astronomers have predicted disaster, and the priests fear the anger of all the gods.

Alexander: If we conquer all of India, we will reach the edge of Asia and take it all. We will be total masters of the world.

Hegelochus: We already are masters of most of the world. We have left our dead on every battlefield from Macedonia and Greece through Persia and Egypt and the lands leading to the gates of India. Let us honor their sacrifices and go home.

Coenus: We refuse, Alexander, to go forward. Our minds are set. We want to see our families.

Alexander: If that is your wish, I will go on alone. You may all turn around and retreat like mice if you wish. I will fight on. I have already made plans to send home the older soldiers who have fought for me even back in the days of my father. A new army is training to replace them.

Demaratus: We know of this army. It is made up of Persians. They are mere boys and foreigners. Who would trust Persians to fight without Macedonians to give them courage? They will run at the first battle like their fathers did. We already have too many Persians and other barbarians in our armies.

SCRIPT: ALEXANDER'S MUTINY (cont.)

Alexander: I understand that you miss home and your wives. Many of you have married foreign wives during our travels. I will make those marriages legal. I also intend to marry a second wife, Stateira, a Persian princess. I have arranged to have 80 Persian princesses brought to our camp when we return from India. We will have a great marriage ceremony and celebration. We will feast for days and honeymoon—after we capture the rest of the kingdoms of India.

Hegelochus: With my luck, I'll get the ugliest woman in Persia.

Coenus: No one minds acquiring another wife until we return home, but the time has come to go home now. We will not go cross that river.

Alexander: I see that I have no choice. I know what the priests and astronomers have predicted, too. I will yield to your wishes, but we will go home by another route. Let us capture the lands we encounter on our journey home.

Narrator: Alexander divided his army into three parts and sent part of it by a water route while he traveled across a very inhospitable desert land along the Indus River to the Indian Ocean. His army engaged in many battles. In one fight, Alexander led his army into a heavily fortified city and was severely wounded. He recovered, but later on the journey, he was bitten by a mosquito and contracted malaria. Alexander died before his army got through Persia. His generals then fought each other for years for control of various parts of his once powerful empire.

READER'S RESPONSE: ALEXANDER'S MUTINY

Directions

- These discussion activities and questions may be used in small groups or with the entire class. They may also be used by the actors as a part of their preparation for the reading.
- Refer to the script "Alexander's Mutiny" when responding to all questions. You may also find useful facts in the background information section, biographies, textbooks, and Internet sources.
- Make notes on the lines provided below each question before your group discussion.

General Discussion

1. Why do you think the soldiers were so angry at Alexander for adopting Persian manners and customs? Did they have good reasons to be angry?

 ____

 ____

 ____

2. Why do you think Alexander's men followed him for so many years before they mutinied?

 ____

 ____

 ____

3. Why do you think Alexander's empire didn't last after his death? Was it his fault, bad luck, or bound to happen?

 ____

 ____

 ____

Making It Personal

Whose position would you support—Alexander or his men who want to go home? Explain your choice.

____

____

____

What is your personal opinion of Alexander's character? Explain your answer.

____

____

____

Would you have followed Alexander as a soldier? Do you admire or dislike his leadership and ambitions? Explain your answers.

____

____

____

ARCHIMEDES' BATH

BACKGROUND: ARCHIMEDES' BATH

Archimedes

Archimedes was born in the independent Greek city-state of Syracuse on the island of Sicily in about 287 B.C. Archimedes was the son of an astronomer named Phidias and was probably a relative of Hieron II, the king of Syracuse. He was well-educated and studied geometry and science at the great library-university complex in Alexandria, Egypt. He returned to Syracuse where he spent the rest of his life. He was a close friend of King Hieron for whom he created many inventions.

Inventions and Discoveries

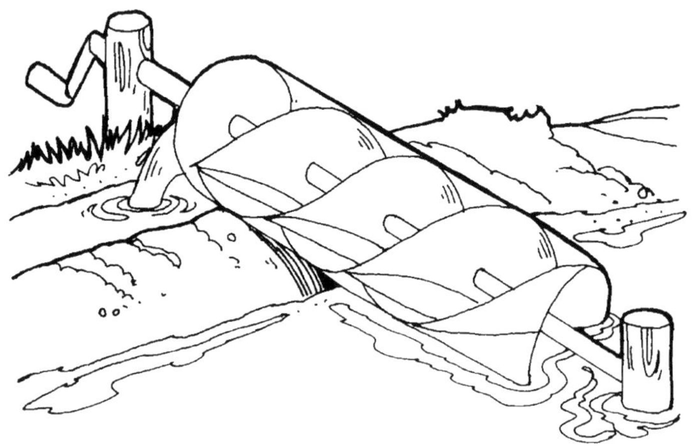

Archimedes is credited with inventing the Archimedean screw, a device that was used to drain lands and irrigate crops in the Nile Valley in Egypt and elsewhere. Versions of this device are still in use today. Archimedes studied the principle of the lever in great detail and bragged to the king, "Give me a place to stand and I can move the world." He invented the compound pulley, a device using ropes and wheels, which could move very heavy objects with minimal force. Using levers and pulleys, Archimedes was able to move a loaded ship by himself. Archimedes also discovered that every object has an exact center of gravity.

Archimedes used these scientific investigations to help him make war machines to defend the city of Syracuse against its enemies, especially Rome. He created a series of giant claws and cranes that grabbed enemy ships out of the water and then sent them smashing back into the water. He is said to have developed a complicated series of mirrors that set fire to enemy ships.

Archimedes studied the properties of water and discovered Archimedes' Principle that explains how buoyancy is created by the upward push of water. He discovered that a floating object displaces an amount of water or other liquid equal to the weight of the object. This was the basis of the proof that the king's crown was made of a cheaper metal rather than gold.

Archimedes was a brilliant mathematician, as well. He studied the surface area of figures, the value of pi, formulas for the surface and the volume of a sphere, and a system of notation for large numbers. His discoveries would later be incorporated into algebra and calculus.

Archimedes died in 212 B.C. during the long Roman siege of Syracuse by the Roman general, Marcellus. Despite the general's orders not to harm Archimedes, he was killed by a Roman soldier in his backyard while working on a geometry problem.

Script Summary: Archimedes' Bath

The setting for this script is the palace of the King of Syracuse in Sicily in the third century B.C. Archimedes, a very famous natural philosopher who studies many facets of life, science, math, and philosophy, runs into the palace fresh from his bath, unclothed, and still wet. He is holding a golden crown and yelling, "Eureka!" (meaning "I've found it!"). The attendants at the court are both amused by his arrival and respectful of his great intellect.

The king had asked Archimedes to prove whether the material used by a craftsman to make his golden crown was pure gold or baser, cheaper metals. Archimedes explains that while in his bath, he worked out the principle of the displacement of water. This scientific concept is based on the insight that every metal has a different mass and that the amount of water displaced is equal to the mass of an object. Gold displaces a certain amount of water. Lead, silver, iron, and other metals each displace varying amounts of water. The king recognizes that the craftsman cheated him and has the soldiers take him away for execution. The narrator concludes with details of Archimedes' fame and death.

Assignment

Read the readers' theater script "Archimedes' Bath." Prepare for the performances and share your interpretations of the scripts with the class.

Extensions: Writing, Science, and Literature

- Write a script based on one of the events listed below or another one related to Archimedes, ancient science, or Greek culture. Use the background section, biographies, textbooks, and Internet sources for help.

  Archimedes develops catapults, giant ship-destroying claws, huge mirrors to start ships on fire, and other weapons to protect Syracuse.

  Eratosthenes measures the circumference of the earth.

  Thales of Miletus discovers the magnetic properties of amber.

  Heron of Alexandria invents many gadgets and instruments.

- Develop a model of any invention or discovery by Archimedes or any other ancient inventor. Use craft sticks, clay, wood, and other materials to make the model. Draw an illustration of the invention and list important facts about it.

- Read any account of the Trojan War, the battle at Marathon, the battle at Thermopylae, or the battles for Syracuse between the Romans and the King of Syracuse between 215 and 212 B.C. Use one episode, chapter, or battle as the basis for a readers' theater script. After practicing your script, share your performance with the rest of the class.

SCRIPT: ARCHIMEDES' BATH

This script is set in the Greek city of Syracuse on the island of Sicily in the third century B.C. Archimedes has come racing into the king's palace unclothed and dripping wet from his bath. There are eight speakers.

Narrator: Archimedes was considered the greatest natural philosopher of his age. He studied many aspects of nature, science, and mathematics. Using mirrors, Archimedes developed weapons that started fires on enemy ships. He is credited with inventing the Archimedes screw that used circular motion to make water rise from a lower level to a higher one so that crops could be irrigated. In this scene, he has just raced to the king's palace from his bath carrying a golden crown.

Archimedes: Eureka! Eureka!

I've got it! I've got it!

I know the answer!

I'm a genius!

Eureka! Eureka! I've found it!

I've found it!

I've got to see the king!

Now!

First Lady: He's found it!

Second Lady: What has Archimedes found now?

First Lady: I didn't know anything was lost.

Second Lady: Well, he must have lost his clothes.

Narrator: The ladies follow Archimedes into the court of the King of Syracuse. There are several other ladies, courtiers, soldiers, and a craftsman with the king.

Paulus: Very poor form, don't you think, Miletus? Even the great Archimedes, favorite of the King, should wear some decent clothes when he comes to court.

Miletus: Indeed, my good friend. It really looks like he left his bath and forgot his clothes. Not for the first time, I might add.

Archimedes: Your Majesty.

King: My friend, Archimedes, the greatest natural philosopher in all of Greece, it is always good to see you.

Did you possibly forget something to wear?

Archimedes: Oh dear, yes, so it seems I did.

King: Well, no matter. I see that you have my crown. Have you solved the problem, friend Archimedes? Is the crown pure gold or has the craftsman cheated me?

Archimedes: Yes, Your Highness. I was in my bath, you see . . .

King: We noticed.

Archimedes: While bathing in the water, Your Majesty, the entire solution came to me in one flash of insight. It was surely a stroke of genius.

First Lady: Everything is always a flash of light with Archimedes.

Second Lady: Yes, but he is brilliant—although he's a little casual about dressing properly.

Archimedes: Let me demonstrate.

Notice that when I dip the crown into this urn full of water, the water overflows.

Paulus: Archimedes has found that water overflows when you put something into it? Even an idiot knows that.

SCRIPT: ARCHIMEDES' BATH (cont.)

Archimedes: You see each material—gold, silver, lead, wood—has a different mass and weight and a different density. So, gold makes a certain amount of water overflow. Silver makes a different amount overflow and so forth.

King: Indeed. Is that so?

Archimedes: This block of pure gold—the same amount of gold supposed to be in your crown—makes this amount of water overflow.

Narrator: Archimedes uses a large urn in the court to demonstrate the displacement of water by the block of gold and the crown.

Archimedes: Observe. When your crown is dipped into the full container of water, much less water overflows.

Craftsman: But, Your Majesty, the shape of the crown . . .

Archimedes: The shape does not matter. Only the amount of gold matters.

King: Does this mean what I think it means?

Archimedes: Your crown, Majesty, is not made of pure gold but rather of baser, cheaper metals as you suspected.

Craftsman: But this is not proof. It is only Archimedes . . .

Archimedes: Your craftsman lied as you suspected. He cheated you!

Craftsman: But . . . but . . . but . . .

Archimedes: I have spent hours in my bath comparing the amount of water moved aside . . . displaced and spilled by gold and silver and the baser metals.

The same amount of gold always spills the same amount of water.

This crown is not pure gold. It is a fake!

Craftsman: Your Majesty, as brilliant as Archimedes is said to be, he may be mistaken.

King: Who else can make water climb uphill?

Who else has invented great pulleys and levers so that two men can move huge objects that would defeat the efforts of twenty men?

Who else has invented great war machines to destroy our Roman enemies?

Craftsman: But, Your Highness, it is only missing a little gold, as you saw yourself. What is so little gold to a man who owns so much?

King: The thief who steals a little will steal more the next time.

Guard!

Narrator: Two armed soldiers position themselves on either side of the craftsman. The King makes a very obvious sign with his hand across his neck. The soldier laughs and puts his hand on his sword.

Archimedes went on to work for the king for many years. He was admired by many kings and leaders of his time. The Roman general who attacked the king of Syracuse and eventually conquered his city gave very specific orders to his soldiers to bring Archimedes to him unharmed. During the battle, Archimedes was working on math problems in the sand behind his home. A Roman soldier was in his light, and Archimedes asked him to move. The soldier killed him.

READER'S RESPONSE: ARCHIMEDES' BATH

Directions

- These discussion activities and questions may be used in small groups or with the entire class. They may also be used by the actors as a part of their preparation for the reading.
- Refer to the script "Archimedes' Bath" when responding to all questions. You may also find useful facts in the background section, biographies, textbooks, and Internet sources.
- Make notes on the lines provided below each question before your group discussion.

General Discussion

1. Which of the characters admire Archimedes? What are their reasons for this admiration?

____

____

____

2. How could you tell if a sword was made of silver or iron? What would you have to know about each metal?

____

____

____

3. Why did the king have the craftsman killed? Was this a sensible or cruel decision by the king?

____

____

____

4. Why were the people at the king's court not upset by Archimedes' appearance?

____

____

____

Making It Personal

Would you like to be a person like Archimedes? Explain your answer.

____

____

____

What do you think was the greatest invention or discovery of the ancient world? Give reasons for your choice.

____

____

____

READERS' THEATER
THE LIBRARIAN

BACKGROUND: THE LIBRARIAN

The Library at Alexandria

The library at Alexandria was founded by the Ptolemy dynasty, the ruling successors of Alexander the Great. It was the brain center of the ancient world, holding more written material than any other place on the earth. Books in the form of hand-written scrolls were very valuable and expensive. More than half a million scrolls, including copies from many languages, were located in this complex which served as a library, a museum containing many scientific discoveries, and a university where scholars from all over the Mediterranean world came to study.

Archimedes, Hipparchus, and Eratosthenes were among the many scientists, mathematicians, and philosophers who studied at the library. Alexandria, which housed this library, was a vibrant center of business and trade. People from many lands and cultures, including Hebrews, Greeks, Nubians, Arabs, and Persians, were living in this cosmopolitan community.

Eratosthenes

Eratosthenes was born in Cyrene in present-day Libya in 276 B.C. He studied under scholars both in Athens and Alexandria, the two great centers of learning at the time. In 240 B.C. he was appointed by King Ptolemy III as the director of the Library of Alexandria where he continued his investigations into many subjects. Among his accomplishments, he measured the tilt of the earth's axis with remarkable accuracy and developed the sieve of Eratosthenes which is a system for determining prime numbers. He also described the fundamental concepts of astronomy in a poem and suggested the use of a leap year every four years to keep the calendar accurate.

Eratosthenes prepared a star map with 625 stars and tried to write an accurate chronological history of the world. He also wrote about philosophy and Greek drama. Eratosthenes was skilled in so many areas of learning that he was nicknamed Pentathlos, a reference to Olympic athletes who compete in several sports. He also had the nickname Beta because he was the second most respected scholar in many fields of learning. Beta is the second letter of the Greek alphabet.

Eratosthenes is especially important for his work as the author of the first major work on geography. He was able to measure the circumference of the earth using his knowledge of science and math. Eratosthenes became blind in 194 B.C. and starved himself to death about the age of 82. He was never married.

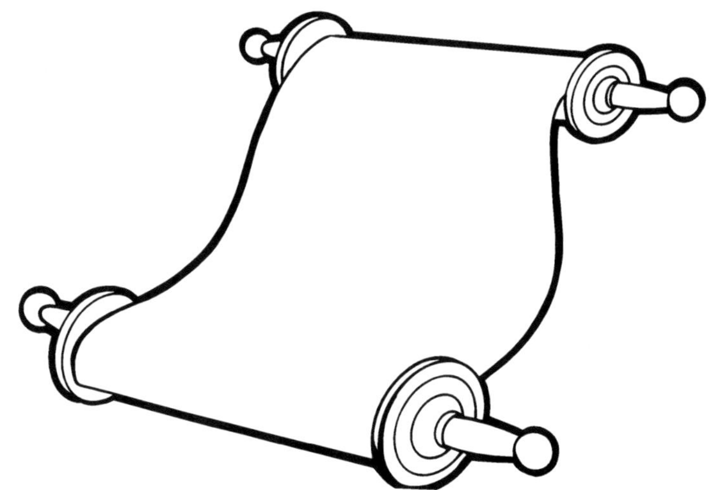

SCRIPT SUMMARY: THE LIBRARIAN

The setting for this script is the great library/museum complex in Alexandria, Egypt in about the year 236 B.C. where Eratosthenes, a highly respected poet, philosopher, mathematician, astronomer, and geographer is the head librarian. Ptolemy III, King of Egypt, is visiting the library that he and his father have spent large amounts of money to build and stock with rare scrolls from throughout the ancient world. His son, Philopater, who is a student of Eratosthenes, is also in attendance as are other scholars and clerks.

Eratosthenes shows King Ptolemy and his son some of the treasures of the museum, including the first dissection drawings of a human, as well as his sieve or design for determining prime numbers. Eratosthenes describes in detail his efforts to measure the distance around the earth based on his calculations and the measurement by bematists (surveyors) of the distance from Syene to Alexandria. Ctesibus, Lysander, and Cleomedes are scholars somewhat amused by Eratosthenes' flattery of the king and his nickname, Beta, because he is the second most famous scholar in several fields of study, although his wide range of knowledge is also acknowledged. The narrator points out that Eratosthenes invented the science of geography and wrote the first book on the subject.

Assignment

Read the readers' theater script "The Librarian." Prepare for the performances and share your interpretations of the scripts with the class.

Extensions: Writing, Art, and Literature

- Write a script based on one of the events listed below or another one related to Eratosthenes or other Greek scholars. Use the background section, biographies, textbooks, and Internet sources for help.

    Eratosthenes describes his sieve for determining prime numbers.

    Eratosthenes and Archimedes discuss science, math, or philosophy.

    Students talk with Eratosthenes about geography or other subjects of interest.

- Use the script or other sources to create an illustration, diagram, or poster of the steps Eratosthenes used to measure the circumference of Earth. Use markers or colored pencils to make the poster attractive.

- Read *The Librarian Who Measured the Earth* by Kathryn Lasky or any other biography about Eratosthenes. Use one episode, chapter, or idea as the basis for a readers' theater script about Eratosthenes' work. After practicing your script, share your performance with the rest of the class.

SCRIPT: THE LIBRARIAN

This script is set in the ancient library and museum of Alexandria, Egypt in about the year 236 B.C. where Eratosthenes, a highly respected poet, philosopher, mathematician, astronomer, and geographer is the head librarian and Ptolemy III is King of Egypt. There are seven speakers.

Narrator: King Ptolemy III of Egypt is visiting the world famous library and museum in Alexandria founded by his grandfather and immeasurably increased by his father. Ptolemy has appointed his son's tutor, Eratosthenes, as the chief librarian. The king's son, Philopator, and three rather jealous officials at the library are in attendance as well.

Ptolemy III: Tell me, Eratosthenes, my chief of this famous library, what treasures have you to show me today?

Eratosthenes: Your Majesty, I am greatly honored to show you the delights of this magnificent library founded by your grandfather. You see here on these shelves countless scrolls containing all the recorded knowledge of mankind since humans learned to write. This scroll is written on animal skins and describes early Greek records of the movement of stars. These scrolls on papyrus are Egyptian records of the Nile floods over many years. There are more than 750,000 scrolls in many languages—Greek, Babylonian, Egyptian, and Sumerian.

Ptolemy III: My customs officials have seized many scrolls and sent them to you. I have paid great sums of gold for others.

Eratosthenes: Your generosity has been like a spring rain flooding us with learning. Our scholars have collected and copied each scroll from every language. Our linguists have translated those of other languages into Greek. The collected knowledge of the world lies on these shelves thanks to your inspired leadership.

SCRIPT: THE LIBRARIAN (cont.)

Cleomedes: *(aside)* Eratosthenes will keep his job for a long time. This king laps up flattery like a cat does milk. Of course, the actual work has been done by poor scholars such as myself.

Philopater: What are these scrolls?

Eratosthenes: These are the first dictionaries listing all the known words in each language: Greek, Latin, Sumerian, Egyptian, and others. This scroll that Lysander is studying contains the collected knowledge of the ancient Egyptians about natural phenomenon. It is one of the first encyclopedias, a collection of all the known truths and ideas about living things.

Philopater: Look at these drawings. They show the insides of people.

Ptolemy III: How were these drawings done?

Eratosthenes: Those are dissections of the human body done by the great doctor, Herophilius. They are the first studies of the internal organs of the human body, dissected from the bodies of criminals.

Lysander: All for the good of science, don't you think, Cleomedes?

Cleomedes: I suppose so.

Philopater: Father, look at this remarkable mathematical design. It was discovered by my tutor.

Eratosthenes: Indeed, Your Excellency, this is one of my favorite discoveries. I am a mathematician as well as a poet, as you know.

Script: The Librarian (cont.)

Ctesibus: Indeed, many of us call him Pentathlos for his many accomplishments.

Lysander: Of course, others have nicknamed him Beta, the second letter of the Greek alphabet, because he is the second most famous scholar in many fields of knowledge from math to astronomy.

Cleomedes: Still, second is better than last.

Eratosthenes: Great King, this is the sieve that I have designed to find all of the prime numbers. Notice how each multiple of two is removed. These are not prime numbers. Each multiple of three and five and seven are likewise removed. Following this pattern will make it possible to determine if a number is prime or composed of other multiples.

Ptolemy III: My son informs me that you have measured the distance around the world.

Eratosthenes: Indeed, Sir, but it was only possible with your magnificent assistance. You have advanced human knowledge immensely.

Lysander: *(aside)* Eratosthenes could flatter the spots off a hyena. He gets more creative in his flattery every day.

Eratosthenes: I am writing the very first book on geography. I found by careful questioning of many travelers across this land that sunlight strikes the bottom of a deep well in Syene in southern Egypt exactly at noon on June 21, the summer solstice. This information has been confirmed by many sources.

Cleomedes: What does sunlight in a hole in Syene have to do with the distance around the world?

Script: The Librarian (cont.)

Eratosthenes: At exactly the same time on noon of June 21, I measured the angle of the shadow created by the sun shining on a pole here in Alexandria. The measurement was 7.2 degrees. This is very important because it is known that the earth is round.

Philopater: How do you know the earth is round? It looks flat to me. If it was round, water would roll out of the seas.

Eratosthenes: No, the earth is round. This has been conclusively proven in many ways. I am also an astronomer, a student of the heavens, and the earth forms a round image during eclipses. Further, when one looks at an object like a tall ship, the first thing seen in the distance is the top of the sail. The rest of the ship comes slowly into view as the ship gets closer. Further, if the earth was flat, the sun would make no shadows because it would hit the earth at the same angle everywhere. Assuredly, the earth is round.

Philopater: I suppose he is right, but it looks flat to me.

Ptolemy III: What did the shadow here have to do with the lack of a shadow in Syene?

Eratosthenes: The earth is round like a circle. There are 360 degrees in a circle. There were 7.2 degrees in the angle of the shadow. I divided 7.2 into 360. This means that the circumference of the earth is precisely 50 times as great as the distance from Alexandria to Syene.

Philopater: But no one knows the distance from Syene to Alexandria.

Eratosthenes: We do now, thanks to the enlightened scientific curiosity of your brilliant father, King of all Egypt.

SCRIPT: THE LIBRARIAN (cont.)

Lysander: *(aside)* Flattery is like butter. It is good in small amounts, but is very greasy if you use too much.

Ptolemy III: It has always been my desire to add to the collected knowledge of the world.

Eratosthenes: I tried to find the distance using the time and distance covered by caravans of camels, but camel caravans travel at different speeds. Camels run away. Desert storms slow progress, and nothing is the same. However, this brilliant king of our people loaned me the services of his most accurate and accomplished bematists. These surveyors of land are trained to walk in exactly equal steps. They walked from Alexandria to Syene. We were able to determine that the distance from Alexandria to Syene is equal to the length of 5,000 stadias. A stadia is the length of a Greek stadium.

Philopater: How did that help?

Eratosthenes: That part was simple multiplication. I multiplied the 5,000 stadias by the 50 parts of a circle. The distance around Earth is 250,000 stadia. I am certain of my calculations. I have dedicated my work to our great king, Ptolemy III, so all people of all times will know of his help in my calculations.

Lysander: I won't believe it until someone measures the earth with a stick. A distance of 250,000 stadia is too large to imagine. It is a huge distance. Who knows what terrible waters and fearsome creatures might exist in a world that large?

SCRIPT: THE LIBRARIAN (cont.)

Eratosthenes: The world is very large and the universe of sun and stars is even more immense. No human will ever know all there is to know. But my book on geography will be a first step to learning about our earth. I have included everything I can find about the lands, rivers, seas, peoples, and creatures of the world. I have traveled from my birthplace in Libya to Athens in Greece where I studied with great teachers. I have written to the great genius, Archimedes, and studied the work of the great scientists who have worked in this library and museum. The sum of human knowledge is infinite. The earth is truly immense.

Philopater: Father, you should see some of these other inventions. There is a water clock here that keeps perfect time and many objects with gears and wheels. From the second level, we can clearly see the great lighthouse in the harbor.

Ptolemy III: Indeed, let us continue our tour.

Narrator: The library and museum at Alexandria was the greatest storehouse of ancient knowledge of science, invention, poetry, mathematics, and literature in the world. It would be a center of learning until it was destroyed by fire about 640 A.D., although many works had already been lost and stolen. Eratosthenes did remarkable work in many fields, earning the nickname Beta because he was the second most famous person of his time in many fields of knowledge. However, he invented the idea of geography as a science, wrote the first books on the subject, and his measurement of the world corresponds to 25,000 miles in modern terms. The exact circumference of the earth at the equator determined by the most accurate modern devices is 24,901 miles. Eratosthenes was only about 100 miles off in his estimate, a remarkable accomplishment. He was a friend of Archimedes and an excellent manager of the great library. Eratosthenes lived from about 276 B.C. to about 194 B.C. He lived to an extremely old age for his time and was growing blind. He voluntarily starved himself to death.

READER'S RESPONSE: THE LIBRARIAN

Directions

- These discussion activities and questions may be used in small groups or with the entire class. They may also be used by the actors as a part of their preparation for the reading.
- Refer to the script "The Librarian" when responding to all questions. You may also find useful facts in the background section, biographies, textbooks, and Internet sources.
- Make notes on the lines provided below each question before your group discussion.

General Discussion

1. Which of the characters did you like best? Explain your choice.

___

___

___

2. Describe the character and personality of two other characters in the script.

___

___

___

3. Why do you think Eratosthenes flatters the king? What does he hope to achieve by his flattery?

___

___

___

Making It Personal

Would you like to be a person like Eratosthenes? What character traits did you admire? Which personal traits did you dislike?

___

___

___

___

What did you learn about writing and knowledge in the ancient world?

___

___

___

What do you think we might know about life in ancient times if the library at Alexandria had never been destroyed?

___

___

___

___

READERS' THEATER
FIRST EMPEROR

BACKGROUND: FIRST EMPEROR

Qin Shi Huangdi

In the year 221 B.C. seven warring states which had comprised China for 255 years were unified by the ruthless tactics of Qin Shi Huangdi (Chin Shee Wang-dee). He conquered the other kingdoms by trickery and by striking his enemies with overpowering military might. He trained farmers to fight in his army and promoted those who showed initiative and bravery. His army used light leather armor and was very fast and mobile. They used swords, spears, and deadly crossbows, which often fired poison arrows. Qin's top government officials were soldiers who had fought with bravery and skill.

Qin imposed an extremely strict legal system with harsh rules and no exceptions. He called himself First Emperor or Sovereign Emperor, but he was more often called the Tiger of China. He imposed a single system of currency and a single Chinese language for writing and doing business. Qin ordered the burning of many priceless books, especially those about Confucius and previous histories because many scholars opposed his excessive authority and his actions that tended to go against Confucian beliefs.

Qin ordered an extensive campaign of building which included a system of roads to connect his empire and the Great Wall of China which he built as a protection against tribal enemies to the north of China. He drafted more than 300,000 peasant farmers to work on the Great Wall and was unforgiving about the tiniest mistake. (The wall in place today was rebuilt much later in the years from 1360 to 1640 A.D.)

Convicts, prisoners, and peasant farmers were among the laborers on the wall and on the First Emperor's most ambitious construction project, his own tomb. This tomb was built over a period of 36 years and covered almost 20 square miles underground. More than 8,000 individual clay soldiers were crafted to accompany the emperor in the after life. Each soldier had a different individual expression. These clay soldiers were arranged in exact military order and armed with real weapons.

The tomb was protected by crossbows with arrows that would be triggered by opening the tomb. All of the people who worked on the tomb are believed to have died or been killed to keep its existence a secret. The outside was covered with grass and looked like a hill. The tomb was accidentally discovered by a farmer in 1974. Peasants revolted soon after Qin's death, and the Han dynasty ruled for over 400 years.

SCRIPT SUMMARY: FIRST EMPEROR

This script is written as a living history documentary in which reporters ask questions of people who lived in another time period. The era being visited is ancient China about the year 211 B.C. when Qin Shi Huangdi (Chin Shee Wang-dee) was the first emperor to unify the warring states of China. Greg and Dana, the two reporters, first interview a sculptor who has created some of the terra cotta (clay) soldiers in the tomb of the emperor. They discuss the remarkable individual expressions, the fine details, the weapons, and the other features of the army waiting in the tomb. The sculptor acknowledges that he will never leave the area and that all of the workers will die when the king dies to protect the secrets of the tomb.

The second interview is with a laborer on the Great Wall of China who explains that he was drafted along with more than 300,000 other farmers, convicts, and prisoners to create this massive structure protecting China from northern tribes who often raided China. The third interview is with a scholar who, like most of his intellectual counterparts, has suffered from the extreme decisions of the emperor to burn most of the historical and religious books (scrolls) in China because scholars have opposed his harsh laws. The announcer concludes with a brief summary of Qin Shi Huangdi's death and the revolts which led to a new Han dynasty.

Assignment

Read the readers' theater script "First Emperor." Prepare for the performances and share your interpretations of the scripts with the class.

Extensions: Writing, Art, and Literature

- Write a script based on one of the events listed below or another one related to life in China during this era. Use the background section, biographies, textbooks, and Internet sources for help.

  A scholar tries to hide some of the sacred Confucian scrolls from the officers of the emperor.

  A farmer gets drafted to work on the Great Wall of China.

  A soldier gets chosen as a model for one of the clay figures.

  A grave robber finds the emperor's tomb after he has been buried for many years.

- Create a small model of a clay soldier from the First Emperor's terra cotta army using modeling clay or art clay purchased from an art supply house. Try to recreate one of the clay figures you find in a book or website.

- Read *The Terracotta Army of the First Emperor of China* by William Lindesay or any other historical account of this emperor. Use one episode or idea as the basis for a readers' theater script about the first emperor.

SCRIPT: FIRST EMPEROR

This script is set in ancient China about the year 211 B.C. when Qin Shi Huangdi (Chin Shee Wang-dee) was the first emperor to unify the warring states of China. There are six speakers.

Announcer: Ladies and gentlemen of our viewing audience, the Living History Channel invites you to join us in a unique virtual journey back into the human past. Today, our correspondents, Dana and Greg, will explore the ancient civilization of China in the year 211 B.C. as Emperor Qin Shi Huangdi, the Tiger of China, is completing the unification of his nation and creating what he hopes will be a long and powerful dynasty.

Dana: We are here at a unique monument in ancient China. King Qin Shi Huangdi became king of the largest of seven warring states that had been battling for more than 250 years. Through the ruthless use of military force, effective administration of his laws, and sly trickery, Qin gradually brought all seven states under his power by the year 214 B.C.

Greg: From the moment he became king at the age of 13, Qin began to draw up plans for his burial tomb. He was extremely concerned about his future in the afterlife. Dana and I are here at a heavily guarded tomb at Mount Li where more than 700,000 laborers, craftsmen, and sculptors have worked for 36 years constructing an amazing underground complex. We have found a sculptor who is willing to answer a few of our questions. Sir, how long have you been here and what is your job?

Sculptor: I have been here 26 years. This is the only job I have ever known. I have helped to construct many of the clay soldiers who will fight for our emperor when he dies and enters the next world. I first learned my skills from a master sculptor for many years before I sculpted my own soldiers from clay.

Greg: Your soldiers are full-sized men made of clay, yet each soldier seems to have an individual face. Some are over six feet tall.

SCRIPT: FIRST EMPEROR (cont.)

Dana: Your clay soldiers are very realistic. There are different kinds of armor and different weapons for each soldier's position in battle. They are even painted in bright colors.

Sculptor: We use models of living soldiers. It is a great honor and a way to accompany the emperor into the next world.

Greg: Why are those loaded crossbows aimed throughout the tomb?

Sculptor: They are ready for the future. When the emperor is brought to the tomb, the bows will be carefully checked and loaded so that anyone who disturbs the tomb will be shot with arrows. There are thousands of swords, arrows, axes, daggers, and spears here for the clay army to use to protect the tomb or accompany the emperor into battle in the next world. Each weapon is ready for use.

Dana: Those buildings look like palaces.

Sculptor: They are smaller models of the emperor's own palaces, some of which have hundreds of rooms. There are also models of many government buildings.

Greg: This underground tomb is huge—stretching over 20 square miles. What are these flowing rivers?

Sculptor: The rivers and seas are made of mercury that represents the waterways of China. They will guide the emperor on his journey.

Dana: The entire roof of this complex shows the stars and planets as seen from Earth.

Greg: When do you expect to be finished and go home?

Sculptor: The tomb will never be truly finished until the emperor dies. None of us will ever leave. I am sure the emperor intends that no one shall ever know the details of his tomb. We shall die here or be killed when he dies.

SCRIPT: FIRST EMPEROR (cont.)

Announcer: The huge tomb of the emperor Qin was not discovered until 1974. He was buried in the tomb, and the workers were probably killed to keep its secrets. Let's return to our reporters in the field.

Dana: We have moved to another massive construction project created by this emperor, the Great Wall of China. Here along a rugged mountain pass thousands of men are digging and packing dirt, moving rocks, and making bricks to support the high wall, its towers, and the roadway along the top of the wall. One of the laborers on this project has joined us. Sir, how did you come to build this wall?

Laborer: I used to be a farmer, but I was drafted by the emperor's soldiers to build roads and this giant wall. I have worked for years building roads throughout the land.

Dana: How many workers are building this wall?

Laborer: Over 300,000 men are working on the wall throughout much of the border between us and the wild tribes further north. We have been working for years. So many men have been taken from the farms to work on the emperor's new roads and this great wall that the remaining farmers have trouble producing enough food for all the people. We are often hungry. Mistakes are not allowed either. If we leave a crack in the wall, we are immediately killed for such carelessness.

Announcer: The building projects of the emperor were incredibly demanding. In a country of twenty million people, more than one and a half million were working on his tomb, this great wall, the roads, his palaces, and other public buildings. Our intrepid reporters have found a scholar in hiding who is willing to talk to them.

Greg: Sir, you seem deeply worried about talking with us. Why do you fear the emperor?

SCRIPT: FIRST EMPEROR (cont.)

Scholar: This has been a terrible age for those of us who want to pass on the light of learning to the next generation. I am old and my days are nearly at an end. I have been in hiding since our emperor demanded the burning of books, many of which have existed for hundreds of years. Our emperor has ordered the destruction of all books, except those about agriculture, medicine, and the supernatural.

Dana: Why did he do such a thing?

Scholar: He has become so dictatorial and so ruthless in his judgments that many scholars of history and the Confucian way of life complained about his violation of family authority and traditional Chinese values. Emperor Qin then demanded the destruction of the works of the great Confucius as well as all historical records. It is a terrible time.

Greg: What are his punishments?

Scholar: Opposition to the smallest rule is punishable by death. He killed more than 460 great scholars in a single year. He killed one of his twenty sons who had opposed his will. The emperor even placed his own mother under house arrest. His philosophy of legalism is rule by strict laws. There is a law for everything and no exceptions are made.

Dana: We have spent some time with three people living in one of the most extraordinary periods of human history.

Announcer: The Emperor Qin had a remarkable career with mixed results. The artistic creations within his tomb are among the most remarkable ever made by human hands. The Great Wall of China is the longest human construction project. Qin imposed one currency and built roads connecting all parts of his empire. He enforced the use of one simplified Chinese language, especially in writing and official documents, but his rule was among the most autocratic and ruthless of all dictators. After his death, one of his sons became emperor, but the Qin family was soon replaced by another dynasty, the Han, who ruled China for more than 400 years.

READER'S RESPONSE: FIRST EMPEROR

Directions

- These discussion activities and questions may be used in small groups or with the entire class. They may also be used by the actors as a part of their preparation for the reading.
- Refer to the script "First Emperor" when responding to all questions. You may also find useful facts in the background section, biographies, textbooks, and Internet sources.
- Make notes on the lines provided below each question before your group discussion.

General Discussion

1. Who did you feel the most sympathy for—the sculptor, the laborer, or the scholar? Explain your choice.

   ____

   ____

   ____

2. Do you think becoming a king at age 13 had any effect on Qin Shi Huangdi's future actions as king? Explain your answer.

   ____

   ____

   ____

3. Why do you think the emperor wanted the clay soldiers in his tomb?

   ____

   ____

4. Did the first emperor help or hurt China? Explain your answer.

   ____

   ____

   ____

Making It Personal

How would you have acted if you were a scholar living under the rule of Qin Shi Huangdi?

____

____

What were the positive aspects of Qin's rule?

____

____

What were the negative aspects of Qin's rule?

____

____

Would you like to be an emperor like Qin Shi Huangdi? Why?

____

____

READERS' THEATER
KIDNAPPED

Background: Kidnapped

A Dying Republic

At the time of Julius Caesar's birth in 100 B.C., Rome, which had been a republic for 400 years, was in the midst of turmoil and internal civil war that had gone on for years. The Senate had once been a group of elder citizens who acted in Rome's best interests. It was now a cauldron of conflict between powerful men who sought power and wealth for their own benefit.

Rome controlled a large empire of many conquered nations. Huge numbers of captive slaves and immense wealth flowed into Rome from these conquered lands throughout the Mediterranean world. Some leaders, like Marius who was Caesar's uncle and a heroic general, tried to provide relief for the poor and distressed people living in the city who did not share in the flow of wealth. Conflicts between powerful rivals led to gang warfare in the streets, chaos in the government, and civil war.

Julius Caesar

Julius Caesar was born to a patrician family of distinction but little money. He became interested in politics at an early age and quickly became an enemy of Sulla, the dictator who controlled Rome at the time. He refused to divorce his young wife, who was from a family hated by Sulla. Eventually, Caesar had to leave Rome for a time with Sulla's agents hunting for him. After Sulla's death, Caesar returned to Rome and began to win appointments to government positions. He decided to go to the island of Rhodes at the age of 25 to become more skilled as a public speaker, a critical skill in moving up the ladder of success. On the journey, he was kidnapped by pirates and ransomed. He gathered a force of fighting men, captured the pirates, and had them crucified.

He formed associations with two rich and powerful Romans, Crassus and Pompey, and became a Consul, the leader of Rome. After this service in Rome, he acquired the authority to raise an army and defeat the Gauls who lived in what is now France. Within a decade, his skills as a general led to total success in Gaul. Caesar returned to Rome with his army and became the dictator of the nation. He defeated Pompey, now his enemy, and eventually became dictator of the Roman Empire. With Cleopatra as a willing ally, he captured Egypt as a Roman province. Caesar had started to institute fundamental changes in Roman government when he was assassinated in 44 B.C. by political enemies.

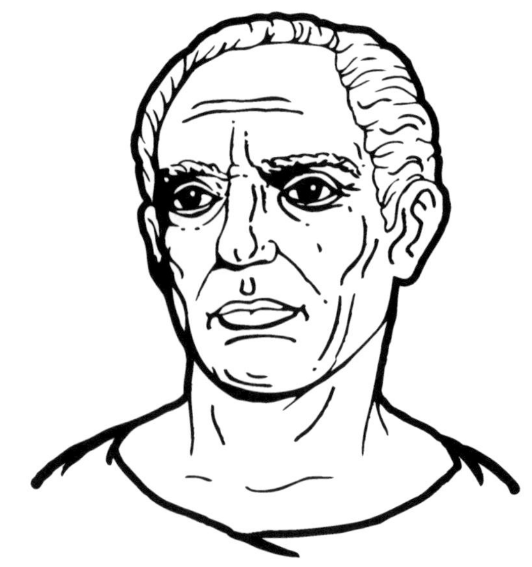

Script Summary: Kidnapped

The kidnapping of Julius Caesar by Mediterranean pirates is the prelude to this script. The young man is brought to the pirate captain who recognizes that Caesar will bring a good ransom from his family and the Roman authorities. Julius Caesar insists that the ransom be 50 talents rather than 20 talents because of his importance. This would equal about 3,000 pounds of silver.

Caesar spends his days in captivity engaging in mock sword fights, foot races, wrestling matches, and the general life of the pirate camp. The pirates enjoy the nerve and good humor of their captive. They regard him as a spoiled but amusing character. The pirates are especially impressed by his audacity when he informs his captors that he will return and capture them. He calmly tells the astounded and disbelieving pirates that, after their capture, he will be required to order their crucifixion. The narrator informs the audience that after Caesar's ransom was paid, he raised an armed force, captured most of the pirates, and did have them crucified.

Assignment

Read the readers' theater script "Kidnapped." Prepare for the performances and share your interpretations of the scripts with the class.

Extensions: Writing and Literature

- Write a script based on one of the events listed below or another one related to Julius Caesar or other important figures of the period, such as Marc Antony, Cleopatra, or Augustus Caesar. Use the background section, biographies, textbooks, and Internet sources for help.

  Julius Caesar crosses the Rubicon and declares war on Rome.

  Caesar meets Cleopatra when she rolls out of a carpet.

  Caesar battles with Vercingetorix or other Gallic leaders.

  Antony and Cleopatra meet.

  Augustus defeats his enemies.

- Read a biography of Julius Caesar such as *Julius Caesar* by Michael Grant or *Julius Caesar: Ruler of the Roman World* by Zachary Kent. Use one episode or a chapter as the basis for a readers' theater script about Caesar's life. After practicing your script, share your performance with the rest of the class.

SCRIPT: KIDNAPPED

This script is set on an island in the Mediterranean Sea in 75 B.C. Pirates have captured a ship carrying a young Roman from an important family, Julius Caesar, and are holding him for ransom. There are eight speakers.

Narrator: Julius Caesar was the son of a distinguished patrician family. His uncle was a famous Roman reform leader and general who had acquired many political enemies in his lifetime. Caesar was ambitious to succeed in a political career. He decided to enhance his opportunities for success by traveling to the island of Rhodes where he intended to improve his public speaking skills by studying with a famous Greek speech teacher. Pirates and other gangs of outlaws were a feared menace throughout the region in this time. Caesar was kidnapped on the trip by a large gang of pirates who often captured wealthy or important people and held them for ransom.

Pirate Captain: Well, what have we here? This young Roman smells of money. See, men, every hair is in place, and he smells of the scents and perfumes of the Roman baths.

Julius Caesar: I am a citizen of Rome. I am protected by the power and majesty of the most powerful republic on Earth. I insist that you release me at once and transport me to the closest city.

Pirate Captain: Would you listen to him? I knew I was right. I can smell treasure in a man. I can tell by your expensive toga and cloak that you are a favored son of Rome. Your family or the Roman government will pay well for your return. In the meantime, you may stay with us and enjoy the small comforts of our island home. They're a little more primitive than you are used to, of course, but you will live—if your people pay. Juba, you can take the note to the Roman authorities.

Juba: How much will we ask for this prize, Captain?

SCRIPT: KIDNAPPED (cont.)

Pirate Captain: We will seek a modest reward, men, for "rescuing" this noble son of Rome. He may someday be a powerful figure, even a man of destiny, in that city bursting with wealth and greed. Juba, request twenty talents for our heroic efforts in returning unharmed this pampered Roman. Those twenty talents will fill our treasure chests with a thousand pounds of silver.

Julius Caesar: This is outrageous! Twenty talents is entirely too little to ask for a man of my prominence. My uncle Marius was a consul and a general. My family is patrician by birth. We have been Roman nobility since the founding of the nation. I, myself, am descended from Venus, the special goddess of Rome. Twenty talents are not enough. You are asking a demeaning, insulting ransom for a man of my birth and breeding. Nothing less than fifty talents is acceptable. The gods themselves will certainly testify to my importance. You could use the silver to keep your camp pleasant for visitors such as I.

Pirate Captain: This is one arrogant son of Rome. Juba, fifty talents it is. We must certainly get a worthy price for this spoiled patrician.

Narrator: The message was conveyed to the Roman authorities in the closest city. It was not an unusual event. Many important citizens of Rome had been kidnapped by pirates before. Kidnapping for ransom was a very lucrative criminal business. While the ransom was being raised by his family and the Roman authorities, Julius Caesar was allowed a good deal of freedom on the pirate island. He spent his time with the pirates and seemed almost to be enjoying his adventure. The pirates spent much of their time practicing their fighting skills.

Julius Caesar: Decimus, you are never going to make it as a warrior if you don't protect your flank. Here, give me your sword. Watch. Felix, attack me. Come at me with your sword.

Slash to the right!

Feint to the left!

Attack the body!

What's wrong?

Felix: The Captain will cut off my head if I kill you or wound you badly enough to die. You're worth a lot of silver on the hoof.

Julius Caesar: You have nothing to worry about. You're not any better than Decimus. Now, just watch as I go through the Roman sword drill.

Slash!

Feint!

Attack!

Whirl to your left!

Protect your flank!

Watch for an opening!

Strike for the legs!

Thrust the sword upward!

Move!

Parry the enemy sword!

Now, let's practice.

Milo: What's the matter, Felix? Can't you whip this spoiled young noble?

Felix: He's good—but he hasn't been cut often enough. Why don't you give it a try yourself, Milo?

Julius Caesar: You both need the practice. Unsheathe your swords. Come at me two at a time. It's good practice for you. A noble Roman is a match for any two outlaws. You, too, Decimus. A Roman expects to be outnumbered—and victorious.

SCRIPT: KIDNAPPED (cont.)

Pirate Captain: We should capture more prisoners like young Caesar. Most of our captives cry and rant or get sullen and depressed. They're so boring I'm glad to be rid of them. Rome can have them back and good riddance. It's a relief to slice off the heads of those who have nobody wanting them back.

Julius Caesar: Milo says you have races. Who is your best runner? I intend to beat him—or are you all afraid to run against this citizen of Rome?

Marcus: No one here has ever beaten me! We go to the tree at the edge of the beach. The loser sharpens my weapons and cooks dinner tonight.

Julius Caesar: I hope that you are a good cook. The food the last few days was fit for a pig.

Milo: On your mark! Go!

Narrator: Caesar won that race and spent the days of his captivity engaging in races, wrestling matches, lifting contests, sword-fighting practices, and bragging, which the pirates did not take seriously.

Julius Caesar: You know, Marcus, you should remain a pirate. You are even a worse cook than your are a runner. It's a pity, of course. I will miss all of you when I have to leave, but I will be back. It's a terrible pity!

Felix: What is the pity, young Caesar?

Julius Caesar: I'm going to have to crucify you, of course. Piracy is punishable by death. The correct method of execution is crucifixion. It's a shame, really. I'm going to regret having to crucify you.

Pirate Captain: You have more nerve than any captive I've ever had. How do you propose to crucify me and my men? Are you going to do it yourself?

Milo: He probably intends to talk us into irons. Well, Julius, do you intend to hang each of us from the cross?

Decimus: He probably intends to talk us to death. I, for one, do not expect to be hanging from some Roman cross. It will take more than this young boy to capture me.

Julius Caesar: I will regret it. I admit that. You have been good company and certainly not boring. But you don't know how to fight. You are unskilled with swords—even on board a ship where you should have an advantage. You don't run well, and you will be easily overwhelmed by Roman warriors. Still, I will regret having to kill you. Nevertheless, justice must be served. I would be lacking in judgment to be merciful.

Pirate Captain: The Roman navy has never laid a hand on me or my men. No Roman authority has control out here. Do you expect to raise your own army and defeat us?

Decimus: They will probably be all rich, young spoiled Roman boys. I hope he brings us some more captives to ransom.

Julius Caesar: Just be warned. You can run away now, if you please, but I will find you and defeat you—much as I will regret it. It is never proper to be too kind or too merciful. I would not want a reputation for being too soft.

Decimus: We're all quaking with fear, young Julius.

Felix: He's either soft in the head or the biggest braggart I've ever heard.

Julius Caesar: Now, Decimus, let me show you how to wrestle like a Roman. It will keep us occupied. My ransom should arrive soon.

Narrator: Julius Caesar was held captive by pirates for forty-two days until his ransom arrived, and he was freed. Caesar sailed to the closest Roman city where he recruited a small contingent of tough men—ex-soldiers, laborers, freed slaves, and adventurers. He offered them the ransom if they would capture the pirates. They succeeded in capturing most of the pirates who were then shipped off to prison. Caesar ordered them to be crucified, the usual penalty for their crime.

READER'S RESPONSE: KIDNAPPED

Directions

- These discussion activities and questions may be used in small groups or with the entire class. They may also be used by the actors as a part of their preparation for the reading.
- Refer to the script of "Kidnapped" when responding to all questions. You may also find useful facts in the background section, biographies, textbooks, and Internet sources.
- Make notes on the lines provided below each question before your group discussion.

General Discussion

1. Which of the pirates did you like the best? Explain your choice.

____

____

____

2. Why did Caesar capture the pirates and order their deaths?

____

____

____

3. Why do you think Caesar spent so much time with his captors?

____

____

____

4. Was Caesar cruel or kind? Give reasons for your choice.

____

____

____

Making It Personal

Would you like to have lived in ancient Roman times? Explain your answer.

____

____

____

____

Would you like to have known Julius Caesar? What were the good things and the unpleasant things about his character?

____

____

____

____

Should Caesar have ordered the crucifixion of the pirates? Explain your choice.

____

____

____

READERS' THEATER
ANTONY AND CLEOPATRA

BACKGROUND: ANTONY AND CLEOPATRA

Battle for Rome: Antony and Octavian

The assassination of Julius Caesar plunged Rome into a period of civil war as various factions vied for power. Mark Antony, an experienced Roman politician, was allied with Caesar's 18 year-old heir, Octavian, against Brutus and Cassius, who had conspired to murder Caesar. After the defeat of these forces at Philippi, Antony and Octavian competed for power in Rome. To cement one agreement between the two men, Antony agreed to marry Octavian's sister, Octavia.

Octavian controlled Rome and the western part of the empire, and Antony controlled the Eastern portion, including Egypt which was a semi-independent ally of Rome. When Antony left his wife and later divorced her for Cleopatra, Octavian had even more reason to fight Antony. Octavian convinced the Roman Senate to fund an army and attack Cleopatra in Egypt. The armies and navies of the two factions fought at Actium on the coast of Greece. For reasons that are unclear, Cleopatra withdrew early from the naval conflict and took her 60 ships to Egypt. Antony saw her fleet leave and soon followed, leaving most of his army behind. Octavian's forces were victorious.

Cleopatra

Cleopatra VII was a descendant of the Ptolemy dynasty that had ruled Egypt for more than 300 years. As a teen, Cleopatra was married to her younger brother, a common Egyptian custom among ruling families, but they soon were competing for control of Egypt. In an effort to win control of Egypt, Cleopatra had herself rolled in a rug and delivered to Julius Caesar who was in Alexandria finishing a Roman civil war. He was enchanted by her and found it good policy to support her in her efforts to control Egypt. They had one son, and Caesar took Cleopatra to Rome.

After Caesar's death, Cleopatra tried to seduce Octavian but was rebuffed by him. She then had an affair with Mark Antony, who later joined her in Egypt and divorced his wife, Octavian's sister. This further inflamed the tension between the two men. Octavian declared war on Egypt knowing that Antony would support Cleopatra. Octavian's victory at Actium made it possible for him to conquer Egypt. The dual suicides of Antony and Cleopatra left him without opposition. He had Cleopatra's son by Caesar killed so that there was no possible heir to the throne of Egypt.

SCRIPT SUMMARY: ANTONY AND CLEOPATRA

The setting for this script is Alexandria, Egypt in 31 B.C. after Mark Antony and Cleopatra have lost the battle of Actium to Octavian, who now controls a powerful army and navy. He is en route to Egypt ready to inflict the final defeat on Antony and Cleopatra. Each of them has tried to negotiate a deal with Octavian who knows he has won and has no intention of losing his advantage. Antony is still angry at himself for deserting his troops and following Cleopatra's ships which had quickly left Actium soon after the battle began.

Antony decides that all he has left is honor and decides to lead his men into battle where he will probably be killed. He wins a skirmish, but his men desert him. Cleopatra goes to her mausoleum to prepare for death as an Egyptian pharaoh might do. Antony is told that Cleopatra has committed suicide, and he falls on his sword which is considered by Romans to be the honorable response when one is beaten in battle and capture is certain. Antony is wounded but not dead when he receives a second message that she is still living and wishes to see him, Antony has his loyal friends carry him to her mausoleum where he dies in her arms. Cleopatra later commits suicide by allowing a poisonous snake to bite her.

Assignment

Read the readers' theater script "Antony and Cleopatra." Prepare for the performances and share your interpretations of the scripts with the class.

Extensions: Writing and Literature

- Write a script based on one of the events below or another one related to Roman history in the time of Antony and Cleopatra. Use the background section, biographies, textbooks, and Internet sources for help.

  The first meeting between Antony and Cleopatra after the death of Julius Caesar

  Antony divorces his wife, Octavia, to join Cleopatra in Egypt.

  Cleopatra leads her ships away from Actium, and Antony leaves most of his troops and follows Cleopatra to Egypt.

- Read any biography of Cleopatra or Mark Antony. Use one episode or a chapter as the basis for a readers' theater script about their lives.

- Read all or part of *Antony and Cleopatra* by William Shakespeare. Write a script of your own in modern English based on one scene from the play. After practicing your script, share your performance with the rest of the class.

Script: Antony and Cleopatra

This script is set in ancient Egypt after Octavian's victory at the battle of Actium. There are three speakers.

Narrator: For almost 14 years after the assassination of Julius Caesar, two men, Mark Antony and Octavian, adopted son of Julius Caesar, contested who would hold ultimate power in Rome. Sometimes they shared power, with Octavian in control of Italy and the western part of the empire and Antony located in the eastern part of the empire. Both men knew that one day they would face each other in a final conflict. The key battle occurred at Actium on the coast of Greece, and Octavian defeated the combined armies and navies of both Antony and his Egyptian ally and lover, Cleopatra. Antony and Cleopatra retreated to Alexandria, Egypt, where they met again.

Cleopatra: Marcus, you did not enjoy the feast or the party tonight.

Antony: Beloved Queen, our time for feasting and drinking is over. Octavian is on the way to Alexandria. He has landed his fleet in Egypt, and his army has begun the march to Alexandria.

Cleopatra: You still have an army to command and I have my fleet, which I saved by leaving during the battle at Actium before they could be destroyed.

Antony: You fled the battle at Actium with your 60 ships, and I left my army. Most of my soldiers went over to Octavian. Your fleet will not fight Octavian's massive armada of ships. I have a small force here, and I intend to face Octavian tomorrow. I do not expect to return.

Cleopatra: Marcus, you remain a Roman to the end. You know that you will be killed. Octavian's army is large, but they are unpaid. Wait until I can raise an army from Egypt and our allies. I have a huge treasury. We will spend it all to defeat Octavian.

Antony: No foreign army has beaten Rome since Hannibal. Octavian has taxed Rome heavily for this assault on us. He knows that the wheat of Egypt and your treasure will pay off the Roman people and his soldiers. I must face Octavian knowing that I will die, but death is preferable to dishonor. I left Actium to follow you. I will not dishonor myself again.

SCRIPT: ANTONY AND CLEOPATRA (cont.)

Cleopatra: Octavian is a ruthless man. I have never been able to reach him. He ignored me after Caesar's death, when I was the most beautiful woman in Rome. I have already offered Octavian huge amounts of money to let us control Egypt or to let me abdicate and leave my children in charge of Egypt, but he kept the money and refused to guarantee our safety.

Antony: How could any man ignore you? I felt the thunderbolt of love the minute I saw you.

Cleopatra: Octavian wants power more than anything. No woman can compete with his desire for power. He hates you because of me. When you divorced his sister Octavia for my love, he saw it as disloyalty and weakness. He will kill our children, and he will march all of us through Rome as prisoners. We must wait and fight when we can win.

Antony: Victory is no longer possible. Death is my only hope.

Narrator: Mark Antony marched his smaller army out to meet Octavian, and he led one brief cavalry charge that pushed back Octavian's mounted soldiers. Then Antony's entire army gradually deserted to the enemy. During the confusion following the battle, Antony received a message that Cleopatra was dead in her mausoleum.

Antony: We are beaten. My last legions have gone over to Octavian. There are rumors that he has already found the great treasure of the Ptolemy kings that Cleopatra intended to use to raise another army. I am beaten on the field of battle. Cleopatra is dead. Life no longer has value.

Narrator: Antony chose to take the Roman way of honor. With a few loyal soldiers in attendance, he fell on his sword, but he did not die immediately. As the blood seeped out of his mortal wound, he received a second message that Cleopatra was still alive and wanted to see him one last time in her mausoleum.

SCRIPT: ANTONY AND CLEOPATRA (cont.)

Antony: My soldier brothers, please take me to Cleopatra's tomb.

Narrator: Loyal aides carried Antony to the queen's tomb. He was lifted through an upper window and lowered to the floor. Cleopatra rushed into his arms.

Cleopatra: My beloved warrior, all is lost but our love. That love must be forever.

Antony: Octavian is on the way even now. I do not want him to see me die in pain. Your love was worth everything.

Cleopatra: I would like to have ruled Egypt like my father before me, but the gods have turned against us. Our love was too wonderful and too sweet.

Antony: Beloved, I die with your beauty in my eyes. All men should be so lucky. Hold me in your arms. Let your hair wipe away my pain.

Narrator: Antony died and Cleopatra made arrangements for her own death. She prepared her body so that it would be ready for burial. She sent away her servants as she heard Octavian's soldiers surround the mausoleum.

Cleopatra: I will not be his slave marched through the streets of Rome for the people to ridicule and spit upon. I will not be the prize shown off to the masses before I am strangled. My beloved Antony, we will be together forever. Neither Octavian nor the gods can deny us.

Narrator: Cleopatra took an asp, a small but very poisonous snake, and held it to her chest. Death was instantaneous. Cleopatra was 39 years old. Her child by Caesar was killed. Her three children by Mark Antony were returned to Rome and brought up as Romans in Octavian's family. With her death, all Egypt became a Roman province.

READER'S RESPONSE: ANTONY AND CLEOPATRA

Directions

- These discussion activities and questions may be used in small groups or with the entire class. They may also be used by the actors as a part of their preparation for the reading.
- Refer to the script "Antony and Cleopatra" when responding to all questions. You may also find useful facts in the background section, biographies, textbooks, and Internet sources.
- Make notes on the lines provided below each question before your group discussion.

General Discussion

1. Why do you think Cleopatra ran away from the battle at Actium? Was it a wise decision?

____

____

____

2. Why did Antony leave his troops at the battle of Actium? Was it a wise decision?

____

____

____

3. Why do you think Octavian had Cleopatra's son by Julius Caesar killed?

____

____

____

Making It Personal

Would you trade the chance to control an empire for the love of a woman (or man) as Antony did? Explain your answer.

____

____

____

____

Who did you admire most—Antony, Cleopatra, or Octavian? Give your reasons for your choice.

____

____

____

____

Do you think Antony and Cleopatra should have committed suicide or kept on fighting until they died? Why?

____

____

____

____

READERS' THEATER
BURIED ALIVE

BACKGROUND: BURIED ALIVE

Pompeii: The Explosion

The small city of Pompeii, located on the Bay of Naples in the Mediterranean Sea on the western side of the Italian peninsula, was a quiet, peaceful place on the morning of August 24th in the year 79 A.D. Around noon, this serene setting was broken by the howling of dogs and the moaning of cattle. The calm waters in the bay suddenly became rough and a stream of smoke lifted to the north off Mount Vesuvius.

A few minutes later, the mountain literally blew its top with a gigantic blast. Smoke, hot gases, clouds of ash, and volcanic stones called pumice exploded into the sky and started raining onto the city. People who had been peacefully buying food at the markets, relaxing at the baths, or working in homes and shops ran in panic to save their lives and their families. Thousands of residents would survive by getting to the ports and climbing on ships that sailed away from the developing disaster.

Other residents would stay because they felt a sense of duty to their employers or their families. Many people wouldn't leave fearing that looters would steal their possessions. Hundreds were killed or injured by the superheated gases, the choking ash, and the falling rocks. Others were injured or trampled to death by people running in blind panic away from the falling buildings and the hail of stones.

The Second Wave

Pompeii housed many wealthy citizens from Rome and many successful merchants and artists, as well as poorer farmers and workingmen. At least one-third of the residents were slaves captured in Rome's many wars or born to slave parents. There were also freemen who had once been slaves. At least 2,000 people stayed hoping to be rescued. Some protected the property of their employers, and others felt they had no place to go.

In the early morning of August 25th, the column of ash and rock fell back onto the mountain and started a gigantic avalanche of ash, pumice, and superheated gases that flowed down the side of the mountain and washed like a gigantic wave over the crippled city of Pompeii and the neighboring town of Herculaneum. People were suffocated by the heat and gases, and both cities were totally buried beneath the avalanche within hours. Pompeii was never lived in again. It was abandoned and forgotten until its rediscovery and excavation in the 19th and 20th centuries.

Script Summary: Buried Alive

The setting for this script is the small Roman city of Pompeii on August 24 in the year 79 A.D. Nearby Mount Vesuvius has erupted. A young boy named Samius is caught in the flood of ash, hot gases, and rocks that are falling on the city. He heads toward the market area to find his sister, Victoria. He meets an older neighbor named Eros who tells Samius he saw Victoria and her dog near the fruit market. Samius finds Victoria with an injured leg and her dog, Perdo, and they walk to the forum for safety.

There they meet an elderly neighbor, Julia, and insist on bringing her along as they make their way to the port, hoping to find a boat which will carry them to safety. On the way, they encounter a wounded gladiator who helps them get to the port, but all of the ships have left. They search through the docks for even a small rowboat but learn that nothing is left. They decide to wait through the night for a returning boat. In the early morning, a new explosion created an avalanche of super-heated gasses and ash that buried the city and killed Samius, Victoria, Perdo, and their friends.

Assignment

Read the readers' theater script "Buried Alive." Prepare for the performances and share your interpretations of the scripts with the class.

Extensions: Writing, Art, and Literature

- Write a script based on one of the events listed below or another one related to the destruction of an ancient city. Use the background section, biographies, textbooks, and Internet sources for help.

  People on a ship watch the destruction of Pompeii.

  Herculaneum, a smaller, wealthy neighboring city of Pompeii, is destroyed by the same explosion on Mount Vesuvius.

  The destruction of the island of Thera in about 1500 B.C. where the lost city of Atlantis was supposed to be

- Create a model of the city of Pompeii or part of the city before its destruction. Include Mount Vesuvius. Use modeling clay, craft sticks, or salt and flour to make the model. Paint the finished model.

- Create a detailed map of the city of Pompeii or Herculaneum with details of the houses, markets, and public buildings. Use colored pencils to illustrate the map.

- Read the short story, *The Lost Dog of Pompeii*, by Louis Auchincloss as the basis for a readers' theater script. After practicing your script, share your performance with the rest of the class.

Script: Buried Alive

This script is set in the small Roman city of Pompeii on August 24 in the year 79 A.D. Nearby Mount Vesuvius has erupted with a massive explosion of ash, hot gases, and rocks that are falling on the city in massive amounts. There are eight speakers.

Narrator: A little after noon on August 24th in the year 79 A.D., the long-dormant Mount Vesuvius had a tremendous volcanic eruption which blew the top off the mountain and hurled thousands of tons of ash, rock, and deadly gases into the sky. The nearby city of Pompeii was suddenly darkened by the choking clouds of ash and gases and bombarded by a blizzard of falling rocks.

People in the small community of about 10,000 permanent residents began to race through the city trying to protect themselves and find their loved ones. Samius is a twelve-year-old boy caught in the midst of this disaster.

Samius: Why are all of the dogs in my neighborhood howling? The sky has turned as black as a thunderstorm at night. There's a fire on the mountain. Smoke is streaming from the mountain. Rocks! The sky is raining rocks!

Neighbor: Get inside, Samius. The falling rocks will kill you, or you will suffocate from the ashes. The mountain has exploded. The gods have been angered. We may all die!

Samius: Victoria, my sister, has gone to the market. I must find her and get her to safety.

Neighbor: Find her and get to the port. You may find a boat that will take you to safety.

Narrator: Samius started running from his home along a crowded street flooded with panicking residents. He raced toward the market. He dodged frantic people screaming with fright, howling dogs, and a barrage of constantly falling rocks.

SCRIPT: BURIED ALIVE (cont.)

Samius: Where am I? I'm lost! I know this city like my own hand. Where is the market? Where is the forum? I have to find my sister!

Older Man: Turn right. I just came from the baths. The city is a madhouse.

Samius: I need a pillow or roof tile to cover my head, or the rocks will kill me. Here's a fallen tile. Run. I have to run. Victoria, find safety until I find you.

Narrator: Samius ran through the streets littered with rocks, falling parts of buildings, and people lying on the streets until he reached the market.

Samius: Victoria! Victoria! Where are you? You should be buying olives and fruit from the market near the temple of Venus. Victoria! It is Samius!

Eros: Samius, get in this building. Where are you going?

Samius: Hello, Eros. I'm looking for Victoria. Our city is being buried. I must find her.

Eros: I saw Victoria and her dog crouched in a corner near the fruit market on the next street. I told her to wait until the rocks stop and then get to the ships in port. They are your best hope for escape. Go find her. I fear the entire mountain will fall on our city. It may be doomed.

Samius: Eros, where are you going?

Eros: I'm going back to my master's house. He freed me from slavery. I am responsible for his home. My daughter, Silvia, is there, too.

Samius: You will be killed there and Silvia, too.

SCRIPT: BURIED ALIVE (cont.)

Eros: Yes, it may be so, but I will die at my duty. It is a matter of honor. Go now, and good luck.

Narrator: Samius raced on through the blizzard of ash and rock and the stench of gases. He hurled himself through the opening of the fruit market and saw Victoria and her dog, Perdo, huddled together in a corner under a wall with part of the ceiling intact. The dog ran to him.

Victoria: Samius, we're here. I couldn't get home. Eros told us to wait here until the rocks stop falling.

Samius: What happened to you? You're bleeding.

Victoria: I fell on the stones in the road when the sky started raining rocks. I twisted my foot, and people stepped on me as they struggled to get away. A rock hit my head, and I went dizzy. Perdo guarded me until I crawled in here.

Samius: Where have the people gone?

Victoria: Everywhere. They have run and staggered and crawled by here in every direction. I think the world is ending.

Samius: I will carry you. Perdo will guide us. We have to get to the boats and get away, or the mountain will fall on us.

Victoria: Let's go to the Forum. That building is strong. We may be protected from the rocks if we go through the Forum and the temples to get near the port.

Narrator: The two young children and the dog began moving through the Forum when Perdo suddenly barks and pulls away from Victoria.

Victoria: Perdo! Come back! Come here!

Samius: He's standing by that fallen woman. Let's go.

Victoria: Perdo! What are you doing?

Samius: It's Julia, our neighbor. Julia, can you hear us?

Julia: Child, what are you doing here? Samius, take Victoria and Perdo. Get to the boats. Leave me.

Victoria: No. Here, lean on us. We're going to the boats. You come with us.

Julia: My old body will only hold you back. Go while you can.

Victoria: We go together. Perdo, lead us.

Julia: Thank you, children. The gods will reward your kindness to a lost and lonely old woman. It is certainly odd to be led by a dog whose name means "Lost."

Victoria: Well, he was lost and found me two years ago. Perhaps we will all have good luck.

Narrator: The two children and the elderly lady followed Perdo down roads littered with rocks and fallen bodies. The ash was already more than a foot deep. They reached the gladiator barracks where they rested for a few moments near a gladiator lying in the courtyard, his sword still in hand. They stopped as the gladiator moved.

Samius: This is Trebius. He won a great fight against two lions just last week. Trebius, can you hear me?

SCRIPT: BURIED ALIVE (cont.)

Julia: Don't shake him. He's a dangerous man. He will just strike at you. You can see he's bleeding from a head wound, and his own sword has sliced his leg.

Trebius: The world is ending. The gods have finally decided to kill us all. Who are you? Where am I?

Samius: The mountain has blown its top. We need to get to the port. The city is doomed.

Victoria: You must come with us now. Julia, tell me how to wrap this sword wound. Perdo is already licking away the blood.

Trebius: The world is ending, and the good spirits have come to carry me away. Come with me. I will get you safely to the ports.

Julia: Look at those two thieves. They are stealing jewelry from that dead woman.

Victoria: Now they're stealing coins from the merchant who is lying next to his shop.

Trebius: They will have no chance to spend somebody else's silver in Hades. The greedy will die here for sure.

Narrator: The gladiator, elderly woman, and two children follow their dog along the roads to the port hoping to find a boat that will take them to safety. In the distance, they can see ships already at sea and riding low in the water. They arrive at the first boatyard.

Julia: Gone! The boats are all gone!

Trebius: We'll look around. There are a lot of other people here waiting.

Victoria: Maybe the ships will empty their load of people and return for us.

Narrator: The group walked through the now crowded wharf looking for a boat and asking questions of the people they met.

Samius: There isn't even a small sailboat or a rowboat. Several of the people waiting came from the other ports along the bay. They're all empty of boats and filled with people trying to escape.

Julia: All we can do is wait. There is no place else to go.

Trebius: It is not likely that any shipowner is going to risk sailing his ship into a port where the sky is covered with clouds of ash and rocks are falling like rain in a thunderstorm. We are doomed.

Victoria: Possibly, but we are together. I have my bag of olives and pears. All we can do is eat and wait.

Narrator: No boats returned that day or evening. That night the column of ash and rock collapsed back on the mountain and a superhot stream of rocks and gas flowed down the mountain creating an avalanche which buried the already ruined city of Pompeii in the early morning hours. The 2,000 people or more who did not make it out to sea were suffocated with the extreme heat and hot ash. Within three hours, the entire city was buried. Samius, Victoria, Trebius, Julia, and Perdo were among those buried.

READER'S RESPONSE: BURIED ALIVE

Directions

- These discussion activities and questions may be used in small groups or with the entire class. They may also be used by the actors as a part of their preparation for the reading.
- Refer to the script "Buried Alive" when responding to all questions. You may also find useful facts in the background section, biographies, textbooks, and Internet sources.
- Make notes on the lines provided below each question before your group discussion.

General Discussion

1. What character traits did Samius demonstrate through his actions?

____

____

____

2. Should the children have helped Julia or gone on ahead? Explain your answer.

____

____

____

3. Why do you think Eros went back to his home?

____

____

____

Making It Personal

Which character in "Buried Alive" did you most admire? Explain your choice.

____

____

____

____

What would you do if you were caught in a massive volcanic eruption or a terrible earthquake?

____

____

____

____

Do you think Eros should have remained behind with his daughter? Explain your response.

____

____

____

____

What one person would you want with you in a disaster? Why?

____

____

____

READERS' THEATER

BELOVED TEACHER AND MUSE

BACKGROUND: BELOVED TEACHER AND MUSE

Hypatia

In 370 A.D., Theon, one of the leading scholars at the Library of Alexandria fathered a girl named Hypatia who was his only child. He deliberately set out to nurture and educate the perfect human. Theon believed that girls were inherently equal in natural ability to boys, but that cultural and social forces kept them from reaching their full potential as humans.

Theon taught Hypatia to read and write, to do arithmetic, and to study the stars and the natural world. In her early teens, she learned geometry, astronomy, and philosophy. Hypatia went to Athens as a young woman to study advanced mathematics, astronomy, and philosophy with Plutarch the Younger and other Athenian scholars.

Hypatia became a scholar and instructor at the library in Alexandria and acquired many students who greatly admired her intellect and her beauty. She was admired by several students who became famous as leaders, including the Christian bishop, Synesius of Cyrene. She was also a friend and mentor of Orestes, the governor of Alexandria. Hypatia was skilled in languages, astronomy, geometry, the developing concepts of algebra, and a philosophy based on reason. Among her inventions was a procedure for distilling drinking water from seawater and an astrolabe used to navigate by the stars.

Hypatia was feared and disliked by the religious leadership in Alexandria. In 415 A.D., she was attacked by a mob probably led by a fanatic known as Peter the Reader. Hypatia was pulled from her chariot, cut to pieces with shells, and burned.

Most of the great library at Alexandria was looted and destroyed by fire in the years after Hypatia's death. Although it had been looted and partially destroyed on previous occasions, the destruction in the 5th century was permanent.

SCRIPT SUMMARY: BELOVED TEACHER AND MUSE

The setting for this script is a quiet park near the great library and museum complex in Alexandria, Egypt in the early years of the 5th century A.D. Hypatia is the leading scholar at this combination library and university. She is greatly respected in the community by many people and feared for her independence and her assertive intellect by others. Among the people who have gathered to listen to Hypatia and her father, Theon, are visiting scholars and leaders, students, citizens, and residents.

The narrator sets the location and introduces the script. Hesychius is a scholar who admires her work. Synesius is a visiting bishop, a former student and friend of Hypatia. Syrius and Peter the Reader disapprove of Hypatia's liberated behavior and beliefs. Orestes is the prefect or governor of the city and an admirer of Hypatia. The visiting scholar represents many scholars who came to talk with her. Theon answers several questions about his decision to train Hypatia as a scholar. Hypatia responds to questions related to her philosophy of life, her mathematical and scientific interests, and her absolute commitment to seeking truth as the goal of her life. The title comes from her students' reference to her as a beloved teacher and to her role as a muse or source of inspiration.

Assignment

Read the readers' theater script "Beloved Teacher and Muse." Prepare for the performances and share your interpretations of the scripts with the class.

Extensions: Writing and Literature

- Write a script based on one of the events below related to the life of Hypatia or the library at Alexandria. Use your imagination and the background section, biographies, textbooks, and Internet sources for help.

  Theon decides to train Hypatia as a child, despite the disapproval of some colleagues.

  Hypatia goes to Athens alone to study with great scholars and meets another young girl scholar.

  Hypatia discusses geometry, algebra, philosophy, or astronomy with her classmates or her students.

  A young scholar falls in love with Hypatia. Hypatia chooses between love and her career.

- Read *Of Numbers and Stars: The Story of Hypatia* by D. Anne Love. Use this picture book as the basis for a readers' theater script about Hypatia. Use the book as a model for creating an illustrated life of Hypatia from her youth to her death at the hands of a mob.

SCRIPT: BELOVED TEACHER AND MUSE

This script is set in Alexandria, Egypt about the year 400 A.D. at a time when women were not considered capable of doing men's jobs or of being educated as scholars. They were expected to become servants or housewives. There are nine speakers.

Narrator: The first great female intellectual of the ancient world was Hypatia, a mathematician, philosopher, astronomer, and natural scientist who was trained to be a "perfect human" by her father, Theon. He did not have a son and decided that girls were as capable of learning as boys. Theon was a respected scholar at the great Library of Alexandria in Egypt, a place that was also part museum and part university. Several visiting scholars from Athens, Constantinople, and other cities, university students, and residents from Alexandria have joined Hypatia and Theon in a small park near the museum where Hypatia frequently lectures and answers questions.

Hesychius: Theon, how did you come to train Hypatia to be a scholar?

Theon: I know that children of both genders are born with great potential. The restrictions of most cultures have forced women to be household servants and obedient housewives. They usually have no other choice in life, but it is a great loss to humanity not to cultivate female minds that are as fertile as the land washed by the Nile River. A girl should be educated the same way as a boy.

Peter the Reader: It's disgraceful. Who does that woman think she is—cavorting around the Great Library dressed in her tribon, as if she was a scholar rather than a woman?

Syrius: Indeed, a woman belongs in the home, not in a school pretending to teach mathematics and philosophy.

SCRIPT: BELOVED TEACHER AND MUSE (cont.)

Synesius: I wouldn't suggest you start an argument with her. Hypatia is trained in several languages, and she is skilled in rhetoric and grammar. She studied with her father here in Alexandria and then went to Athens where she was educated by several brilliant scholars, including Plutarch the Younger. She can debate the nature of life or the principles of Euclid's geometry with equal ease. Her books on natural science, geometry, and astronomy are skillfully written and very learned.

Peter the Reader: She belongs in the kitchen and the nursery taking care of her children and preparing meals for a husband. It is unnatural for a woman her age not to be married long ago.

Orestes: Believe me, she has had many offers. Her father allows her to choose, and she does not intend to be any man's servant. The world might be better if more women were so independent.

Syrius: It is not right for a woman of her beauty to deny herself of a man. She should choose a rich husband.

Hesychius: Hypatia will never be obedient. She believes that each human has an inner voice which tells us what to do. She follows her own inner voice.

Syrius: But she doesn't believe in any of the gods. She doesn't follow the ancient Greek ways or the new ways of Christians. She has no god.

Synesius: My friend Hypatia is a Neoplatonist. She believes in what she sees and experiences, not what she is told that cannot be proven. She believes in the power of reason.

Hesychius: It must be lonely to have no god to ask for help.

SCRIPT: BELOVED TEACHER AND MUSE (cont.)

Scholar: Hypatia, do you believe that all of geometry and math has been discovered?

Hypatia: No, my father and I have written books explaining the principles which Euclid discovered about geometry, but there is far more to learn. I wrote a book focused on the remarkable features of cones. There is no end to the discoveries yet to be made about math.

Scholar: But surely, we know the ways of the stars and the other heavenly bodies.

Hypatia: There will be many more worlds and wonders to discover in the cosmos. What we don't know and have yet to learn will fill more books than this great library at Alexandria now holds.

Hesychius: What is your favorite branch of mathematics?

Hypatia: I am especially fond of studying the new branch of mathematics dealing with unknown quantities that has developed from the work of Deophantus. It extends the power of mathematics beyond geometry and arithmetic into an entirely new realm of thought.

Syrius: How did a woman manage to design an astrolabe for navigating the oceans by fixing the positions of the stars in the sky?

Hypatia: By studying.

Scholar: How did you learn to distill fresh water from sea water?

Hypatia: By trying one method after another until I found a system that worked. Discoveries are made by diligence and hard work. They do not float into the mind like dust on the air.

SCRIPT: BELOVED TEACHER AND MUSE (cont.)

Peter the Reader: Who would need this water taken from the seas?

Hypatia: Sailors are often stranded for weeks on the sea in the blazing sun without a source of drinking water. Egypt has had many droughts, and thousands die each time from the lack of water.

Hesychius: The Jewish synagogues in this city have been burned by mobs, and there is a lot of religious feuding between Christians and those holding other beliefs. Do you hate the Christians or other religions?

Hypatia: I respect everyone's right to believe what their minds tell them. I have many Christian friends including bishops, one of whom, Synesius, was my student.

Synesius: Indeed, I value your friendship, Beloved Teacher. But I fear for your life in these difficult times of political and religious unrest.

Hypatia: One's life is always at risk. I intend to live my life learning all that I can about the world I inhabit.

Orestes: But my friend, as the governor, I know that your life is in danger from those who fear your influence.

Hypatia: Even if my life is in danger, what good is it to live a life of fear—a life one does not choose to live?

Peter the Reader: Why don't you wear proper woman's clothes? The tribon you wear makes you look like a man, a scholar.

Hypatia: I am a scholar.

SCRIPT: BELOVED TEACHER AND MUSE (cont.)

Peter the Reader: You drive your chariot through the streets of our city like a soldier or a man of wealth and power. At least hire someone to drive you. It is not proper for a woman to drive a chariot.

Hypatia: What is proper is not always what is right. I do not choose to have others do my work. I think for myself, and I drive for myself.

Syrius: Why do the authorities discuss the great problems of the day with you?

Orestes: Let me speak to that. I am the prefect of Alexandria. I value the mind and the intellect of our beloved teacher. She is a muse who opens minds that are often closed by hatred or ignorance.

Synesius: I am the Christian patriarch of Cyrene, but I greatly value Hypatia's insights. She learns by thinking freely. One must admire that. She seeks wisdom and loves truth.

Hypatia: This advice I give to all—leaders and priests and common people. Reserve your right to think, for even to think incorrectly is better than not to think at all.

Peter the Reader: But where is your true faith and allegiance? Are you Greek or Roman or Egyptian? Are you pagan or Christian?

Hypatia: I enjoy the ancient stories of Greek battles, the gods in their heavens and on our world, and the adventures of heroes from many lands. But I do not believe them to be true. Superstition is the enemy of truth. To teach a superstition about any god of the past or present as truth is terrible.

Peter the Reader: But you must believe in something.

SCRIPT: BELOVED TEACHER AND MUSE (cont.)

Hypatia: I believe in truth—truth that is rational and proven. The truth must always be sought after. Truth is the greatest goal of life.

Syrius: Didn't your father influence your beliefs? Don't you believe what he believed?

Hypatia: My father taught me to ask questions. I learned to accept no answer that could not be proven by examination and questioning and observation. I do not accept any dogma, the set of beliefs of any idea about the earth or the heavens or a god that I cannot analyze and understand and prove.

Peter the Reader: Why have you never married? If you married a scholar, your sons might become great scholars.

Hypatia: As a philosopher, I am married to the truth. My heart is wedded to the Supreme Good, the most noble rules of life and honor.

Orestes: Beloved teacher, do you think there will always be evil in the world?

Hypatia: Evil exists, but it does not have to exist forever. Man is capable of not doing evil and of overcoming evil.

Narrator: Hypatia was to experience that evil when she was murdered by a mob led by Peter the Reader. She remains a symbol of the power of the human will to seek knowledge and truth despite all obstacles.

Reader's Response: Beloved Teacher and Muse

Directions

- These discussion activities and questions may be used in small groups or with the entire class. They may also be used by the actors as a part of their preparation for the reading.
- Refer to the script "Beloved Teacher and Muse" when responding to all questions. You may also find useful facts in the background section, biographies, textbooks, and Internet sources.
- Make notes on the lines provided below each question before your group discussion.

General Discussion

1. Do you think Hypatia would still face some criticism in today's world? Explain your answer.

2. Which of Hypatia's accomplishments did you find the most admirable? Why?

3. Why do you think Syrius and Peter the Reader were so negative in their attitude toward Hypatia and her father?

Making It Personal

Did you admire or disapprove of the character and personality of Hypatia? Explain your response.

Do you think that it is possible to nurture and educate the "perfect human" as Theon tried to do? Explain your answer.

Do you think boys and girls think and learn in the same way? Give several reasons and examples in your response.